THE ROAD TO FORGIVENESS

BILL AND CINDY GRIFFITHS

THOMAS NELSON PUBLISHERS®

Nashville

To Robyn and Janice

CONTENTS

PART 3: THE WAY

PART 4: FINDING OUR WAY

PART 5: THE ROAD TO FORGIVENESS

ACKNOWLEDGMENTS

Our first praise must go to Jesus for the work He has done and is continuing to do, deriving good fruit from a horrific calamity. Without Markus Wilhelm asking us to write this story, there would be no further need for acknowledgments. For his vision, determination, and most of all, friendship, we are forever grateful. We are extremely appreciative to Michelle Rapkin, a passionate servant of God and us. Michelle was responsible for coordinating everything and everyone, as well as brainstorming and lubricating the entire development of this book from day one. This book was very difficult for us to write, and Michelle held our hands through it all.

We are indebted to our children, Stephen, Luke, Willy, Peter, and Summer, for their help, love, and understanding whenever this project derailed us from seeing to their immediate needs.

We would also like to thank our editor, Judith Marcum, for a hard job well done, and Barbara Greenman for the fine details that make a book a book.

We are grateful to Brian Hampton, Kyle Olund, and the team at Thomas Nelson for their enthusiasm and hard work. And finally, we thank Roger Cooper, Mel Parker, Andrea Doering, and all those working behind the scenes at Crossings for their time and support.

To contact us, go to www.wggriffiths.com.

PART 1

CALL HOME IMMEDIATELY

CHAPTER 1

SAYING GOOD-BYE

(CINDY)

Summer vacation! For a mother who home-schools her six children, that season is especially welcome. When Monday morning, June 24, 1996, dawned bright and clear, I was more than ready for it. The first week of summer vacation.

Our children, too, were eager to begin their summer adventures. Stephen, who was almost thirteen, was staying home in New York to work with Bill for the summer as a carpenter-in-training. Luke, our nine-year-old, had left the day before for a week of summer camp in Pennsylvania. Willy, Peter, and Summer, our seven-, six-, and three-year-olds, were starting a week of vacation Bible school, a church day camp filled with songs, crafts, and games focused on the development of the children's relationship with God. I was left home alone for a few hours with our eleven-year-old daughter, Robyn, who would be leaving the next day for a month-long trip to the West with my parents.

Robin had the choice of going to camp at Victory Valley with Luke for a week or taking the trip with her grandparents. She loved camp, but my parents would be traveling to Salt Lake City, where two of my brothers, Joe and Rob, lived. Robyn loved spending time with her cousin Aspen, my brother Joe's daughter. And in two weeks, my brother Rob was getting married out there. In fact, Bill, Summer, and I would be meeting them at the wedding. So after some quiet deliberation, Robyn chose the trip with Grandma and Grandpa.

In a way, I didn't want Robyn to go. A month was a long time for her to be away. But how could I deny her the trip? Not only was she eager to spend time with her cousin, but she was being afforded the educational opportunity to see new places and have new experiences. Being the home educator that I am, I saw that as a definite plus. Besides, it was what she wanted to do, and my parents were thrilled to have their oldest granddaughter traveling with them on the trip.

Before I knew it on that sunny Monday, it was time to pick up the little ones from vacation Bible school, have lunch, and get Robyn to my parents' house in Franklin Square, about a half-hour drive away. They were leaving early the next morning, so Robyn was spending the night with them.

At my parents' house, the kids played in the yard, and then we had dinner. As daylight slipped away, I asked everyone to come into the living room for prayer. We all held hands, even my dad who "wasn't into those things," and we prayed for safety, protection, and blessing during their travels.

I gave Robyn a long hug and kissed her. I had talked with her about the magnificent panorama she was going to see when they reached the Rocky Mountains. When I was fourteen, I had driven through the Rockies with my family, and I still remembered how enchanted I had been with their natural beauty and majesty. I had always hoped that I would get to see those magnificent mountains again someday.

Now I bent over so I was at face level with Robyn, and pretending to be serious, I said, "When you get to the Rockies, I want you to scan your view of them, north to south, or south to north, it doesn't matter. But you can't blink while you do this. Then you have to shut your eyes tight for the rest of the trip. When you come home, we'll set you in front of the wall in the family room. Then you can open your eyes, and the scene of the mountains will be projected onto the wall." Then I added, "For my eyes long to see what you're going to see."

When I was sixteen, God became real to me for the first time in my life. He became a person to me, not a religion. Not a set of principles to live by, but a person with a personality, thoughts, and feelings. Someone reachable, a close and loving friend. I came to know Him as the One who knows all things. If I had a problem I couldn't solve, I could go to Him, confident that He would lead me in the best possible way.

Over the years, as my life became busy with the many responsibilities of mothering, I learned to set aside time, however minimal that might be, to spend alone with God each day. My friendship with Him had become a dependency. I wanted to be the best mom I could be, but sometimes life got so hard, so exhausting. I often sang songs to Him and meditated on Bible passages, soaking in His love for me, and my strength was renewed. Then I'd bring problems, big and small, to Him.

As I grew older, I began to imagine the day when I'd step out of time and into eternity. And sometimes in the quietness and solitude of my early morning visits with God, I would close my eyes and imagine what it would be like to live completely free of my inner struggles and the difficulties of life to rest in the presence of ultimate beauty, joy, and unconditional love. And I'd whisper, "Oh, how I long to be where You are, Lord. My eyes long to see what You see."

I had said it often. Now, for some reason, I used those exact words as I said my good-byes to Robyn. Then I reminded her to keep up with her journal writing. I requested an entry a day.

Five minutes later, while I was talking with my parents, she came over to me and hugged me. She'd been unusually quiet, and I asked her if she was all right, if she was having second thoughts about the trip.

"No, Mommy, I'm fine," she said.

A few minutes later as I was winding down my conversation with my parents, Robyn approached me again. She gently placed her arms around my waist and held me. I was definitely concerned. If she didn't want to make the trip, I was not going to force her. Despite all the planning, preparation, and anticipation, if she really didn't want to go, she would not go.

Her face was nestled into me as we embraced, and I pulled back just enough to take a thoughtful look at her sweet face, at the sun-kissed freckles splashing across her nose and cheeks. Gently, but firmly I asked, "Robyn, are you okay? Are you *sure* you want to go? You don't have to if you really don't want to."

Her big, kind chocolate-brown eyes were full of peace as she held me tight and softly assured me, "Mommy, I'm okay. I just want you to know that I love you."

Her words and her demeanor put my mind at ease. Little did I know that would be the last time I'd see my beautiful daughter in this life.

CHAPTER 2

THE NIGHTMARE BEGINS

(CINDY)

Friday, June 28. Robyn and my folks had been on the road for four days, and they had called every day. But today I did not hear Robyn's sweet voice over the phone. Instead, I heard my brother Scott.

After lunch, I had taken our son Willy to the pediatrician in Glen Cove. Several minutes into the examination, one of the office staff came in and said that there was an emergency phone call for me and that I could take it on the phone in the examination room. It was Scott.

"Whatever you're doing, drop it and come home immediately," he said in a monotone voice that was very uncharacteristic of my fun-loving younger brother.

"Why, what's the matter?"

"Just come home."

"Scott, what's wrong?" I demanded.

"Cindy, just drop whatever you're doing and come home."

"What is going on?" I said impatiently.

"Just come home."

"Okay, I'm coming."

I hung up and faced the doctor. "I hope everything is all right," he said, looking concerned. Then he gave his diagnosis of Willy's problem.

I remember seeing his mouth move, but I didn't hear anything he was saying. My thoughts were flying, spinning. *Gotta get home. Gotta get home. What's going on? Gotta get home.*

On the fifteen-minute ride home, I kept thinking that maybe my grandmother had died. She was over ninety, and her health had been declining rapidly of late. Still, that wouldn't warrant an emergency phone call. And Scott had called from our house. Momentarily I wondered, *How'd he know where to find me?* Oh, yeah, Stephen was home mowing the lawn. Stephen must have told him. But something was wrong. Scott sounded strange—serious and distant. What was going on?

Then I did what years of Bible study and time spent with God had taught me. I knew that the more God filled my vision, the more He would crowd out my fears. So I began to sing songs about God's saving power and about His love for me. No matter what was awaiting me, God's love was greater still.

As I drove, I sang, and my singing was solemn, the words mouthed carefully and deliberately as if they were a weapon I was using to protect myself against danger. In essence, I was building a shield of faith.

CHAPTER 3

CALL HOME IMMEDIATELY

(BILL)

I was in East Northport, almost an hour away from home, when my beeper went off. It was the third time my pager had beeped in the last five minutes. The other two numbers could wait until I got off the roof, but not this one. It was our home phone number. Our son Willy had been experiencing unusual tenderness, and Cindy was taking him to the pediatrician today. Although it probably had something to do with the aggressive way he played, always coming home with torn clothes and cut knees and elbows, the idea that something serious might be wrong had lingered with me all morning. The page was probably from Cindy, wanting to tell me I could stop worrying.

I used the phone in the customer's kitchen, and it was answered on the first ring. To my surprise, it wasn't Cindy or even one of the kids. It was my brother-in-law Scott, and he was telling me to sit down. His voice bore no resemblance to his usual jovial nature.

"I'm sitting," I said.

He breathed heavily two or three times before speaking. Suddenly I was nervous.

"There's been an accident," he said, obviously straining to get the words out.

I was silent, too nervous to speak.

His voice started breaking up as he said, "Grandma didn't make it."

Grandma didn't make it? Scott and Cindy's grandmother was about ninety years old and in a nursing home. I was instantly sorry that something had happened to her. Cindy would be upset. But what kind of accident could happen in a nursing home?

"And there's more," he said, laboring to breathe between pauses.

What more *could there be if she died?* I wondered.

"Robyn didn't make it either," he said. He could hardly get the words out. "Robyn died in the crash. They were . . ."

Scott continued to talk, but my racing mind shoved itself away from what my ears were hearing. I didn't scream. I didn't cry. I didn't speak. I couldn't. I suddenly felt as if someone had just emptied a shotgun into my chest. He hadn't been talking about his grandmother at all. He was talking about his own mother, Cindy's mother, my children's grandmother, his children's grandmother.

My thoughts flailed about in a desperate search for threads of hope to hold onto. The threads I found were like cobwebs, vanishing at the slightest touch of reason. He wouldn't joke about something like this. His message was too simple to have been misinterpreted. He could be speaking of only one Robyn. *My Robyn.* I was getting weaker by the second from this strange weight, this pressure that seemed to be rapidly increasing all around me.

"Bill . . . are you there? Are you all right?" Scott asked.

"Yes," I said, my voice sounding to me as if it was coming from another person. My head began to rock forward with each deep breath. "Does Cindy know?"

"No," he said, coughing and choking. "I called her at the doctor's office and told her to drop whatever she was doing and come home."

"How did you know she was at the doctor's?"

"Stephen told me."

"He's with you?"

"Yeah."

"He knows?"

"Yeah."

"How is he?" I asked, knowing the answer.

"Not good."

"Don't leave him, Scott. Whatever you do, don't leave him," I said. I was nearly an hour away. If only I could be there right now. *I need to be there right now.*

I bolted out of my seat, sending the nails in my tool belt pinging onto the tile floor. Halfway to my truck, I met Angelo, one of my workers. I didn't want to tell him anything. I had no time to. Even if I had the time, I don't think I could have gotten the words out of my mouth. Sensing that something was wrong, Angelo followed me to my truck.

"Are you coming back?" he asked as I opened up the rear roll-up door of the truck.

"No," I said. Then with a sudden burst of anger, I threw my tool belt as hard as I could into the back of the truck and slammed the door down twice before latching it.

I was furious. Although I love my brother-in-law Scott, I hated him at that moment. History is full of dead messengers, and now I know why.

Once out on the street, crushing the gas pedal, I screamed,

"Robyn, Robyn, my baby, nooo, baby, Robyn," again and again. Tears poured and poured, and her face filled my mind as I drove through every red light for the next twenty-five miles. With both hands on the steering wheel to support my weakness, I passed every car on the road.

"Why?" I cried out to God. "Where were You?" I screamed, angrily blaming Him for her death. However it happened, God could have prevented it.

Furious at God, I remembered prophecies spoken over me at church that proclaimed protection. Powerful promises that had strengthened my faith over the years suddenly infuriated me. Just then I remembered a prophecy that had been spoken over me just a week ago—a prophecy that had frightened me as soon as I heard it, spoken by a woman known for her prophetic accuracy. "I will make you a comfort." When I first heard the words, I thought, *Thanks, but no thanks*. To be a comfort to someone in need, the person has to know that you can relate to his suffering from your own experience. It was at this point that a revelation flooded my mind and turned me around 180 degrees.

Willy!

Willy was supposed to go on the trip, too, but didn't. I started thanking God with all my heart as loud as I could for Willy's life.

I allowed the thought that Willy was alive to capture me for as long as it could. But the battle between anger and thankfulness soon continued. In my pain I wanted to cling to God, and in my pain I wanted to be distant.

Fresh thoughts of Stephen handling this news with neither Cindy nor I there to hold him compelled me to stand on the throttle. And what about Cindy? Was she home yet? I hoped not. I desperately needed to be there when she heard the news.

CHAPTER 4

A Knife in My Heart

(Cindy)

When I arrived home, I flew out of the car and saw Stephen coming toward me. He looked sullen and said I needed to talk to Uncle Scott because something bad had happened. I raced into the house.

Scott was in the kitchen. He looked more serious than I had ever seen him. He told me to sit down. I wouldn't. He gently but firmly pushed me into a chair. Then he said, "There's been an accident."

Accident? It was as though I didn't know the meaning of the word. My mind was blank. Something very dark descended upon it.

"And?" I questioned, rising from the chair. It was too confining.

"Dad's okay."

What is he talking about, Dad's okay? What does that mean? My family was in an accident? They were in an accident? Oh, God, what's he talking about, and why didn't he say Robyn was okay? All of this shot through my mind in a split second.

"And?" I demanded, my eyes wide. Scott began to cry, yet he held my gaze.

"Mom died," he said.

I grabbed his arms. *"And Robyn?"* I was almost yelling.

"She died too." His voice crumbled under the weight of his words.

A mighty force, like a volcanic eruption originating in the center of the earth, came up through my feet and out my mouth. "Noooooooooo!" I screamed.

I had to run. I ran out the front door and up the street. I don't know if it was the mighty surge of anguish pushing me to do that or a desire to run away from what I had just heard. It was probably a combination of both. I ran around the corner and saw my neighbor Richie on his porch. He asked me what was wrong. A moment later Pat, the mother of Robyn's friend Tori, came out into the street toward me, asking what was the matter. My mind was on fire as I repeated my brother's words to them. We crumpled together in a heap in the middle of the road. Scott was there in a flash, and I was yelling, "No, oh, my God, no!" But there were no tears. Not yet.

I don't know how long we remained there, but when I looked down the sunny suburban road, I saw Bill's van.

CHAPTER 5

HOME

(BILL)

As I turned onto Walnut Street, a block away from our house, I saw Cindy jumping hysterically in the middle of the street. She was flanked by three neighbors who were trying in vain to embrace her. I passed them, turned the corner, and pulled into the driveway. No sooner had I stepped onto the pavement than Stephen ran into my arms. I crushed his head tightly to my chest, imprisoned in a common nightmare, sensing he needed to know that I was alive as much as I needed to know that he was.

Cindy ran into the driveway, crying, screaming, "This didn't happen! This didn't happen!"

I reached for her with one arm and held onto Stephen with the other. I didn't know what to say after hearing Cindy's cry echo my own. The thought of no longer seeing Robyn's beautiful smile or hearing her happy voice was too painful to endure, but too looming to escape. I don't know what my mind would have done if I hadn't had a wife and five other children who desperately needed me not to crawl into a dark corner and disappear. I didn't want to think. I didn't want to exist. There was nothing in the world I wanted or would ever want, except to see Robyn. I wished I were dead. Then the pain would stop, and I would see Robyn.

I pulled Cindy and Stephen tightly against me so that the three of us would be as one. Maybe that would help.

"No, no, no!" Cindy screamed, erupting in my arms, then bouncing on her tiptoes. "I have to move. I have to move," she said. She began running laps around our front yard. Three other women, all neighbors who knew Robyn, cried and ran after her, not wanting to interfere with what they could not understand but unable to simply watch.

Suddenly Scott was there, the messenger who had delivered the devastating news. My irrational anger toward him was smothered by his quick embrace. Overwhelmed by my own loss, I needed to remember that Scott had just lost his mother in the same accident. I told him I was sorry, but his blank expression as well as Cindy's cries—"Robyn, Robyn, Robyn"—clearly divided the expected from the unexpected, the natural from the unnatural. As tragic as losing a parent is, there is a natural order that seems thrown to the wind when a child dies.

With Cindy screaming and running and collapsing, friends and neighbors running to her, huddling around and hugging, Cindy breaking away, not wanting consolation, screaming, jumping to her feet, running, screaming, collapsing to her knees again, I pleaded with Scott to explain to me what had happened.

"How did it happen? What do you know?"

CHAPTER 6

A Heart On Fire

(Cindy)

I don't remember going back to our house, but I do remember Bill holding me in the driveway. His eyes were wet, and I could see the shock on his face that must have been a reflection of mine. I remember him embracing me, and I remember pulling away and starting to run again.

I ran and ran and ran.

I did laps on the front lawn until I tired, but the minute the smallest twinge of energy returned, I ran and ran again. In exhaustion I'd let Bill hold me, but then I'd be off running again. I don't know how long this went on.

I remember people, Bill's arms, running, and pain.

My heart and mind were burning up in a fire of ruthless white-hot flames, and there was nothing to quench it.

PART 2

WHERE DO WE
GO FROM HERE?

CHAPTER 7

A Drunk Driver

(Bill)

Scott didn't have much information, but what he did have, he remembered exactly. As he told me what he knew, he paused to exhale after every few words, as if he had just run five miles.

A doctor in Nebraska, who had found Scott's beeper number in his father's wallet, paged him. The doctor began by telling him that there had been a car accident about an hour ago and that his father had suffered a concussion and broken ribs; he was pretty beaten up, but stable. Scott immediately imagined his mother huddled with Robyn in some emergency room; he could see his mother asking every passing nurse for a moment-by-moment update on her husband's condition. But the doctor's next few words severed Scott's mental image as effectively as an executioner's ax. His mother was dead. Then, mercilessly, the next blade dropped. Robyn was dead.

Later, when delivering the news to Stephen and then to me and finally to Cindy, Scott followed the same pattern the doctor had used, each blow all but eliminating the one before.

Scott answered my next question before I could ask it. The doctor said that Robyn hadn't suffered. Part of me was relieved and thankful, but most of me still didn't want to accept that she had died.

Although the news of Robyn's death ran me over like a train, my thoughts of her being dead were more like bayonets rammed to the hilt, thrust into my chest and abdomen. I couldn't understand how Cindy could be running when all I wanted to do was to fall into a fetal position and die.

Scott then told me that the doctor said that alcohol had been involved.

What? This was not simply an accident? A drunk driver was involved? In the morning?

I wanted to go to my safe and get my shotgun. I wanted to jump into my Jeep, bury the throttle and slam every gear, crash through the hospital doors, smash through the wall, and blow the drunken killer's head off. Even the fact that the crash had happened two thousand miles away was not insurmountable. I could take my shotgun to the airport and catch the next flight to Nebraska, *then* blow the killer's head off. Everyone would understand. Even the security people at the airport who were scrupulously searching carry-on baggage through X-ray monitors would wave me through as soon as they were apprised of the situation. They would probably be helpful. On second thought, probably not. Forget it. I'd buy a shotgun there. That would delay me only a few minutes. As unrealistic and detached as these psychotic thoughts sound to me now, they seemed totally rational at the time.

I needed someone to think for me. Someone who knew me and Robyn. Someone close who could take control of the situation. Take control of me. I thought of my parents. But they were in New Hampshire, three hundred miles and six hours away. My brother Craig. He was living in Massachusetts, only four hours away. But I needed someone now. My good friend and lawyer Mark Eskenazi. No, he had gone upstate with our pastor to speak at some church in Kingston. If I could only get in touch with him, he would come back immediately, but how could I get in touch with him? I was in no shape to even think of how to track him down.

There had to be a way to hide from all this. If only I could climb into a wall and ask someone to seal it up behind me. Maybe all this would go away if I could get into a wall. *But I can't. I'm needed.*

The front door behind me opened. I turned to see who it was and was immediately embraced aggressively by a medium-sized man with thick, slicked-back glossy hair. *Mark Eskenazi!* Somehow, he had gotten the news just before he was ready to leave and had rushed over to our house. I thanked God for Mark's presence as we both cried uncontrollably.

I wasn't so blind with my own distress that I could fail to see how ripped up Mark was. His daughter Lauren and Robyn were best friends, and Mark had spent countless hours driving the girls to ballet, ice-skating, church meetings, beaches, and wherever else the two dynamos pleaded to go. Some of Mark's tears were for Cindy and me, but most of them were for Robyn, a little girl who was like a member of his own family.

Crying became the norm. If I wasn't crying at any given moment, I would be soon. The jabbing, stabbing reality of Robyn's death saturated every thought. I searched and searched for a loophole. There must be some way to bring her back. She was too young, too full of life, too good a daughter, too good a person, too loving to others, too . . . Robyn. *Dear God, this can't be true. It has to be a huge mistake.*

An hour later friends and relatives and neighbors filled our home. Neighbors I hardly knew were embracing me in tears. Children of all ages were inside and out, some weeping alone, others grieving together, huddled like clumps of wilting flowers. Every few moments the screen door opened for someone else who had just heard the news. Many begged me to tell them it wasn't true. And although a common refrain was, "I don't know what to say," people were pouring love like salve on the gaping wounds that we were.

Mark disappeared into my office to gather whatever information he could from the hospital and the police department. The details we had received thus far were brief and sketchy, and as the facts unfolded, I wanted Mark to filter them for us.

Before long, he called Cindy and me and Scott into the office. He had just been on the phone with the Nebraska authorities and the hospital.

. . .

"Do you think you can hear some details?" Mark asked, wiping his swollen eyes.

None of us could answer.

"Look, I'll do whatever needs to be done to make this painful process a little less painful, but I'm going to have to make you aware of some things so you can tell me what to do."

"Tell us whatever you think we should know," I said. "We trust you completely."

"Well, I'll start with your father," Mark said. "He's in the intensive care unit, but he's stable and conscious. They want to do some more testing, but so far it looks like he's going to be all right."

"Does he know?" Cindy asked, gripping my hand tightly.

Mark nodded, then went on to tell us that Janice and Robyn never knew what hit them and hadn't suffered.

"And the other driver?" I said.

"A few bumps and bruises . . . nothing serious. They say she had a point one-nine blood alcohol content. Twice the legal limit."

"How did it happen?" I asked.

"From what the police can surmise, your folks were stopped on the side of the road, and she hit them in the rear. The police said that sometimes a drunk will use a car in front of her to confirm to herself where the road is. When they stopped, she didn't. There were no brake marks."

"Why did Joe stop?" I asked.

"They don't know yet."

"What's her name?" Cindy asked.

"Verma Harrison. She's Native American."

There was a pause, then Cindy asked, "Do you know anything else about her?"

"She's thirty-five."

"Is she married?" Cindy asked.

"I don't know."

"Does she have children?"

"I don't know."

"Where was she coming from? Where was she going?"

"I don't know."

"What will happen to her?" Cindy asked.

"She'll be charged with murder. I'm not sure how that works in Nebraska, but I'll find out," Mark said.

CHAPTER 8

MAD AT GOD

(BILL)

I suppose that I must have been in some kind of denial because hearing the word *murder* reinforced the reality that Robyn and Jan had died. The word also roused my anger again. I still had visions of grabbing my shotgun, but my target had changed. I wanted to find something valuable. Something that I owned. Something that I enjoyed. Something that I had worked hard for. Or better yet, something that God had given me. The Jeep I've taken care of the last eleven years, the computer I write on, my fish tank, the television— the whole house that I had built with my own two hands. I would blast the whole world to bits, including myself, if it would help turn back time.

At that moment, though gripped by the deepest anguish I had ever known and frustrated that no amount of rage would accomplish anything, I heard God knocking on the door of my mind and quietly whispering, *I am with you.*

Part of me didn't want to answer, while another part of me did. I knew perfectly well what God was trying to do. He wanted me to have faith that He would work everything out for the good, and He wanted me to forgive the woman who had just killed Robyn.

Objectively I believed that, but internally I wasn't ready to listen. Not yet I wasn't. I wanted God to know that I was mad at Him. There was no sense in not being honest with God. Whatever the facts were, He had allowed the crash to happen. He had allowed it. I had endeavored to make God my top priority for the last twenty years, and He had betrayed me. I didn't want to embrace God; I wanted to embrace my shotgun. Pump, fire, pump, fire, pump, fire, fire, fire, fire . . .

I am with you.

I had known God as a faithful comforter in times of trouble, but right now He could keep His comfort. He had protected *me* so many times in the past. Why me and not Robyn? I'm selfish, easily insulted, argumentative, self-centered, impatient, insensitive, egotistical, and more. Robyn was compliant, helpful, loving, fun, and sweet. If You love Your creation, God, why did You take Robyn and leave me here?

I am with you.

How could this have happened? They were in Nebraska on an empty highway at seven-thirty in the morning. What was this woman, a guided missile? An asteroid with Robyn's and Jan's names on it?

I had to wonder if there was a purpose behind God's allowing it to happen. But what purpose could justify taking Robyn from us? Why couldn't God figure out another way?

The first thing I was taught in writing class was that your main character needs to want something. If he doesn't want something, you don't have a story. Everybody wants something. Even God. My belief is that God wants two things: (1) a love relationship between us and Him and (2) a love relationship between us and us. Everything God does has something to do with those two wants. But at this point, I wasn't interested in trying to figure out what God wanted. I just wanted this news not to be true.

· · ·

Mark was still handling all the phone calls and messages, so when Cindy's father called late in the afternoon, Mark came to get us.

Joe's injuries weren't serious, but they were painful. And even greater than his physical pain, he was suffering the emotional distress of having lost his wife and granddaughter, and the guilt of being the driver, even though the accident was not his fault. His last words to Cindy before leaving Long Island had been reassurances about Robyn's safety. "Don't worry," Joe said. "I won't let anything happen to her."

"Joe's afraid to talk to Cindy," Mark said. "And he's terrified of talking to you."

I grabbed the phone. "Joe," I said, "I love you. We need you." I told him to get back here as soon as he could because we needed him here.

He was a sobbing mess, unable to say anything other than, "Bill, I'm so sorry. I'm so sorry. Little Robyn . . . Jan . . . I'm so sorry, Bill." In response, I kept telling him that I loved him and I wanted him to come home.

Then I handed the phone to Cindy, and after some similar dialogue, she asked the question we'd all been wondering about: "Why were you on the side of the road?"

CHAPTER 9

SUPPORT

(CINDY)

My parents had left Ogallala, Nebraska, early that Friday morning, heading west on Interstate 80. They intended to stop for breakfast in Wyoming. It was almost seven-thirty and they were several miles east of the small town of Sidney, Nebraska, when they noticed a car on the right shoulder of the road. The driver was a woman, and she had several children in the car.

My mother suggested they stop and offer assistance, and my father pulled his minivan onto the shoulder of the road, intending to back up the quarter mile or so to the car. My dad had slowed down and was almost stopped when they were rammed from behind by a van traveling at an estimated speed of eighty-five miles per hour. They were hit in the right rear corner, sending the minivan over the two highway lanes and well into the center median. The minivan was crunched like an accordion up to the back of the front seats.

Robyn had been stretched out on the middle seat with her headphones on, listening to a tape. They needed the Jaws of Life to get her out.

The impact was so great, Robyn and my mom were gone immediately. My dad had been unconscious and had been taken to a hospital in Sidney. He had a concussion, four broken ribs, and neck injuries. (Although I am telling what happened as I now know it, it actually took days, even weeks, to get all the details of the accident.)

Dad couldn't tell us all this at the time. He was still sedated, so his words were slurred, and he could barely get out a complete sentence. I could hear him straining to breathe through his tears. He kept saying my name and Mom's name and Robyn's name again and again. Then he asked me, "Why am I still here? Robyn should be here, not me."

Oh, how I hurt for him. I was upset that he had been told about my mother and Robyn before someone from the family was with him. But apparently Dad had asked about them as soon as he regained consciousness, and the doctors had told him they were gone. More than anything, I wanted to comfort him, so I told him the things I had been starting to comfort myself with. I told him that Mom and Robyn were with God who loves them and that they were not in pain. In response to his question about why he was still alive, I pulled no punches. I told him that Mom and Robyn were ready because they had accepted God into their hearts. The way to heaven was wide open for them. He, however, was not in that same position. He had been given another chance to do that.

About two or three weeks before their trip, my mother's church had performed the play *Heaven's Gates, Hell's Flames*. In it, several scenarios depicted what happened after physical death. As the characters died, they appeared before an angel who had the authority to look into a book that the Bible calls the Lamb's Book of Life to see if the new arrival's name was written in it. If it was, the person was permitted to enter heaven's gates, where he was greeted by none other than Jesus Christ. One character in the play was a mother who, after entering heaven's gate, was reunited with her little child who had gone before her and was holding Jesus' hand.

Some of the characters found that their names were not written in the Book of Life. They were not permitted into the Creator's presence, but were escorted away to a place devoid of love and joy and peace and loved ones.

I asked my father if he remembered that play. He said yes. "That's what I mean, Dad," I told him. "Mom's name and Robyn's name are written in the Lamb's Book of Life. Spiritually they were ready to go." I asked him if he was ready now to make that commitment. Was he willing to allow God into his life?

"Yes," he said.

I began to pray for him and with him on the phone. Actually I did most of the talking, but he either acknowledged or repeated what I said. During this bittersweet moment of extreme vulnerability and sorrow, I hoped my father's heart was genuine, responding and not just reacting to the moment. Only time would tell.

When I hung up the phone, I wanted to jump on a plane and be with my father. The thought of him in a hospital, wracked with pain and not knowing a soul, added to my torment. Whatever physical injuries he had sustained would not compare with the emotional trauma he was experiencing.

I was comforted to know that my brothers Ray and Scott (who live here in New York) were preparing to fly out there immediately. Before the day ended, family would be at my dad's side. I kept thinking, *I love you, Dad. I love you, Dad.*

· · ·

A sea of faces flowed through and around our house that afternoon and evening. Mark and Linda Eskenazi and their daughter Lauren, one of Robyn's good friends. Mark seemed to be able to step in for Bill in all kinds of practical ways. Though it was painful for him, too, Mark faithfully handled phone calls to and from Nebraska, trying to determine what had happened and what was going on out there. The burden of relaying the crushing information to us lay heavily on his shoulders.

Robyn's friends came to the house. Those poor kids. They just wanted to take care of their friend. (We later learned that Tori and a group of girls went door to door telling the neighbors about what had happened to Robyn and asking for contributions for her funeral.) With tears, I confidently told them that Robyn was okay, and that they, too, could have eternal life and play with her again someday. I encouraged them to keep God first in their lives.

Along with reassuring others, I told myself again and again that my mother and Robyn were all right. They were with the One I loved more than anything in this world, and "in His presence is the fullness of joy." But the thought of never seeing them again as long as I lived here on earth was absolutely unbearable.

For the most part, I felt like a walking corpse—as though all the life had been drained out of me, as though I wasn't even there. I felt as though I had been punched so hard that all of what makes me *me* on the inside was sent off into space somewhere far, far away. Yet a lifeless corpse wouldn't feel pain, and I certainly felt pain. I was concerned for my children, but I couldn't even comfort them. I saw them being taken care of by others, and I rested in that.

As the day darkened into night, my friend Elaine asked me what I needed. I didn't know what I needed except one thing—to get before God.

Over the years I've made a practice of reading the Psalms every morning. Now my mind reflexively went to Psalm 23:

> The LORD is my shepherd,
> I shall not want . . .
> He leads me beside quiet waters.
> He restores my soul . . .
> Even though I walk through the valley of the shadow of death,
> I fear no evil; for Thou art with me. (vv. 1–4)

If ever I was in a valley of death, it was now. If ever I was in need of having my soul restored, it was now. If ever I was in need of the tranquility of a quiet mountain pool, it was now. My Bible said not to fear because God was with me—even in the midst of the storm raging inside me. I needed to spend time with God, focusing on Him and allowing Him to warm and fill my vision. He was in the valley with me. He would come to my aid.

Psalm 27 also came to mind:

> The LORD is my light and my salvation;
> Whom shall I fear?
> The LORD is the defense of my life;
> Whom shall I dread? . .
> Though war arise against me,
> In spite of this I shall be confident . . .
> For in the day of trouble He will conceal me in His tabernacle . . .
> He will lift me up on a rock.
> And now my head will be lifted up above my enemies around me . . .
> I would have despaired unless I had believed that I would see the
>   goodness of the LORD

In the land of the living . . .

Be strong, and let your heart take courage;

Yes, wait for the LORD. (vv. 1, 3, 5–6, 13–14)

As I had done in the car earlier, I wanted to sing songs that would call to mind who the Lord is. I desperately needed His comfort, so I told Elaine that I wanted people to worship with me. I wanted guitars, and I wanted to sing praises to the One who is worthy of all praise. The One who could help me. I wanted to be in the presence of the One who promises to draw near to us if we will draw near to Him.

By that time, Bill and I had retreated to our bedroom. My head was pounding, and my eyes were swollen from all the crying. I tried to seek some relief in the unconscious realm of sleep, but I don't recall whether or not I dozed. I do remember that people came into the room, and some brought guitars. Our friends started singing softly. So did I. And as I sang those songs, filled with the truth of the Scriptures, I began, once again, to be reminded of God's love for me.

I sat on my bed, rocking to and fro in time with the music. I prayed out loud, pleading with God to heal the hole in my heart.

When Robyn was born, the physical pangs of labor had engulfed me, causing me to focus on small inanimate objects, to breathe rapidly and walk a tightrope that stretched over a canyon of mind-snapping fear. The pangs of death were encompassing me now, only unlike birth, there was nothing to look forward to, just to what had been. I needed to focus on what would bring me through the turmoil of this mental hell, looking not to the left or to the right, but to the truth that would lighten my darkness.

Sometime later, a friend said that I reminded her of a woman in labor that night. I had brought Robyn into the world, and now I had to let her go. I had to let her be born, through her death, into another world. In both her birth and her death, there was anguish for me, and in both there was birth for Robyn. Birth and life. The first birth for only a short season of life, the other for eternity.

Gradually peace began to flow over me, and I experienced some respite for my soul, even if it was only for the duration of the time spent focused on God. As long as I could keep worshiping, I had a place to hide in the storm.

. . .

(BILL)

That night our house was filled with people, as it had been all day. Friends and relatives dropped everything in their own lives to care for us. If I left them for as much as half a minute, even to go to the bathroom, I felt their absence like missing air to my lungs and had to return to their midst as soon as possible. I recognized that their love was an extension and provision of God's own love, grace, and healing for us. But I still felt betrayed. God wouldn't have had to heal us so much if He hadn't allowed this awful mess in the first place.

About twenty people huddled with us in our bedroom, half a dozen of them surrounding Cindy and me on our bed. My good friend and pastor Dave Harwood led us in worship and praise with my guitar.

For the last twenty years I had been taught, and had in turn taught others, to praise God in all situations, to call on His name in the time of need. One of my favorite verses in the Bible was in the book of Job. In the midst of having lost his children and all his belongings and being plagued with disease, Job still proclaimed, "Though He slay me, yet will I trust Him" (13:15 NKJV). At my side,

Cindy appeared to embody those words. Lost in God's presence, she sang His praises from her heart. But right now, praising God was a struggle for me.

We were heartsick and weary, yet neither Cindy nor I wanted anyone to leave. And as wasted as we were, neither of us could sleep. Our nightmare kept our minds too busy to rest. I held Cindy close. I had lost my daughter and my mother-in-law, but she had lost her daughter and her mother and her two best friends. I wanted to somehow fill the void, but I knew I would fall short.

· · ·

(CINDY)

Bill and I and our friends sang into the night. The kids were tucked into bed, and several of the women stayed and slept downstairs in the living room in case we needed them in the night. They did that for several nights.

I was so exhausted, I wanted to sleep, although I doubted that I could. But even more, I wanted to be alone to talk with God. I went into the bathroom and knelt down on the floor, sitting back on my heels. During the day I had been crying out in pain, like a child who is seriously injured and cannot be comforted. Now I was quiet.

Thoughts of never seeing my daughter again, of what that would be like, ricocheted off the walls of my mind. I wanted to die. This was bigger and blacker than anything I had ever experienced, and there was nothing I could do to change what had happened. Part of what makes a tragedy what it is, is this sense of overwhelming, unrelenting helplessness.

There in the bathroom in the dark, save for the moonlight coming through the small skylight overhead, I climbed onto my Father's lap and poured out my heart to Him. Unlike my earlier tears, these tears flowed with words that were for His ears only. He listened. He understood. He had compassion on me. He was gently cradling every thought in His hands, saving every tear. And in that place of knowing such compassion, I believed that God had a purpose in allowing this situation to happen.

Some say that everything happens for a reason. That everything that happens is God's will. I don't believe that. God never intended for evil desires and acts to run rampant on the earth. But I do believe that He will use even evil things for our good *if we trust Him.*

I began to think about the power of God and to speak aloud of His greatness. I confessed with resolution, even defiance, in the face of mortality, that His power was stronger than death. Sobbing, pounding the floor, I shouted my thanks that because of God's great salvation, Robyn and my mom lived, and I would live with them again.

The fire raging within me began to be vented through my prayer. Though I longed to have my daughter back, I beseeched the God of the universe to use this disaster for good. "You are the Author not of death, but of life," I cried. "Like the seed that must fall to the ground and die in order to grow and bring forth life, let their deaths bring forth life in others. Many others."

Then, battle-weary, I went to bed and fell asleep in Bill's arms.

CHAPTER 10

SHADOW OF DEATH

(CINDY)

Saturday morning I awoke early, unrested and heavy with grief. I dragged my sleep-deprived body into our walk-in closet and sat down on its two steps, a usual custom for me in the early morning. I opened my Bible to Psalm 57, which is a prayer for deliverance. When the psalmist first gave voice to these words, he had an enemy army pressing in upon him. I could relate to his plea for help. I could also relate to his confidence in God for the deliverance that was yet to come. But I still felt like a prisoner weighed down by the enemy's chains. My mind was the prison and my grief the shackles. My breathing was shallow and labored, as though I needed more oxygen, more space.

As the sun was coming up, I went outside and pulled a few weeds from the flower beds in the backyard. It was a beautiful morning. The air was still and clear, with none of the nasty humidity so typical of Long Island summers. Sunlight dappled the ground, filtered through the huge oak tree in the adjacent yard. The purple clematis climbed the front of my little garden shed, creating a wonderful contrasting backdrop for the orange-and-salmon Tropicana roses. The scent of roses filled the corner of the yard. I smelled them. I touched them. Yet I could not enjoy them. Then I looked at the two-by-eight-foot flower bed that was Robyn's, and the tears flowed.

Just three weeks before, we had planted the garden together. Near winter's end we had begun studying my gardening catalogs, planning and scheming about how we would lay out the garden. I remembered teaching her the meaning of the word *perennial* the day we planted. And I remembered how she was especially looking forward to seeing blooms on the lavender Angel Face climbing rosebush she had planted in her garden.

I have always encouraged the children to grow something in our vegetable patch. Actually I required it. It became a seasonal home-school project. Now that Robyn was eleven, she was developing her own appreciation for nature's bounty and wanted a piece of earth to call her own, not just a row in the small family vegetable garden. I enjoyed sharing this project with her—and the fact that something that blessed my heart became her enjoyment as well. I loved sharing things with Robyn. I loved giving to Robyn. I loved watching her *become*. I loved being Robyn's mom. *I didn't want to stop being her mom.*

All these thoughts pierced my heart like a hot knife. My time to give to her had come to an abrupt end. No longer would we be able to get excited over a newly blossomed bud. No longer would we talk of flowers together. No longer would we play on the trampoline with each other. No longer would we sing our favorite songs, dance in the kitchen, bake or sew, read or laugh or argue, or do *anything* together.

I wouldn't get to watch her practice ballet and see how graceful she was becoming. I wouldn't see her snuggling with her three-year-old sister on the couch, reading to her. I'd never see her riding her bike again, blowing out her birthday candles, or sitting at the table doing her schoolwork. I wouldn't hear her clown around with her brothers or make my piano sing. I wouldn't see her reach her sweet sixteen, graduate, get married, or hold her own baby. She was gone. My daughter was gone. She'd never be back. She'd never walk this earth again. *I didn't want to stop being her mom.*

Then I heard the voice of God within me, reminding me of the word I had taught Robyn just a short time ago. *Perennial.* Only this time I did not think of it as defining the life of a plant; it defined the life of a young girl. Robyn's life was like a perennial flower. A flower that blooms for a season—a short season compared to other blooms—and then appears to die. Indeed, part of it does die. The part that we see. Yet the part that we cannot see, the part that is hidden—the root—remains alive, only to cause the plant to grow again and bloom at another time.

Robyn, too, had bloomed here on earth for a season, for a short time. Then the part that we saw died. But the part of her that made her who she is—her spirit—still lived, and she would bloom again at another time and in another place. Heaven. My daughter—God's perennial flower. The thought of her alive and well with Him stilled some of the tempest within me. God was alive. He had conquered death. And because He lived, I *would* live with Robyn and my mom again.

"O Lord," I whispered, "I don't want to think anymore. It hurts too much . . . I am here, Lord . . . I still walk in this place . . . You let me continue to be here, but how can I go on with all of this raging in my mind? I can't . . . I don't know how to think anymore . . . Show me how to think . . . Where do I go from here? 'You will keep in perfect peace him whose mind is steadfast, because he trusts in you,'" I quoted from Isaiah 26:3 (NIV). "How can I be steadfast in You when I can't see You through all of the thick, dark clouds? Direct my thoughts because I just don't know how to think anymore."

All at once, in my imagination, I saw myself working the soil on a farm. My hands were on a plow, and I was walking forward, pushing and guiding the plow, which was fastened to an animal. The plowing was hard work. But I needed to *keep moving forward* if good things were to come—the harvest. There were many good things yet to happen in my life too. I needed to press forward, to lean into the work, hard though it was. Yes, there was still a plan for me. God was still going to cause new things to grow in my life for Him. I wanted to continue to follow Him until He called *me* home.

The picture of the plow set my mind on what is *yet to be.* I realized that if I spent all of my energy looking back at what I *could not* have, I would be missing out on the present and the future.

CHAPTER 11

DAY 3 . . . SUNDAY

(BILL)

Two days had passed since the crash. I was still wandering around like a zombie, stunned and in shock, not knowing where I was going or why I was going there. I was unable to focus on anything but my devastated world. My last words to Robyn returned to me again and again: "I really, really love you." And hers to me: "I really, really love you, too, Daddy."

A window of objectivity had opened, allowing me to at least recognize that my sarcastic attitude toward God was reactionary and wrong. But I had never experienced such a dichotomy between emotion and faith. I couldn't discern where my heart ended and my head started.

We hadn't left our home since Friday, since we got word of the crash, but it was Sunday morning, and we were going to church. Getting into our Chevy Suburban, we walked smack into a wall of reality. The vehicle that was bought to provide enough seating for

Cindy, me, and the six children was suddenly—and I mean *suddenly*—too big. Robyn's seat was very obviously and painfully empty. When one of the children innocently sat there, I almost told him to sit somewhere else. Cindy, who was determined to get to the church meeting and let the heavens know that God was still in control, had tears streaming down her face.

At that time our congregation met in a rented space on the second floor of a small mall. I've been a member of this congregation for the last twenty years, since I first came to know the Lord, and the important thing about our worship has always been *why* we gathered, not *where*. But when I walked through the single glass door and into the dark blue carpeted space we've called the Center for the last three or four years, the atmosphere was gray lead, heavy, totally foreign to any other time I had been there. The shotgun blast that had emptied into my own chest had apparently also emptied into the chests of many others. Robyn had been known and loved here. She was not just a member of our family. She was a member of everyone's family—this family of God.

Rich and Cathy Cicarello were the first to greet us. They, too, had lost a daughter to a speeding drunk driver. In 1987, Maryann, who had had nothing to drink, was in the passenger seat of an old white Chevy sedan when the intoxicated driver failed to negotiate a right-angle turn on their way from a beach party. A few days later, Rich and Cathy visited the guy in the hospital to tell him that they had forgiven him. When I first heard what they had done, I wondered whether I could ever forgive under such circumstances. I didn't think I could. I tried to imagine one of my own children in Maryann's place. The thought was so horrible that I couldn't dwell on it but a moment. Now the unimaginable was here.

The choice that Rich and Cathy had made to forgive rather than hate was tougher for Rich than for Cathy. He had battled with the question *why?* They were also criticized by some, who openly wondered what kind of cult they were involved with that they could forgive such an act. Rich and Cathy had done the right thing in the eyes of God, if not the eyes of man.

All the way to our seats, people grabbed us and hugged us, Cindy and the children and me.

The evening before, right after we had answered "definitely" to the question of whether we would be at the Sunday morning church meeting, we were asked if there were any particular songs we wanted to use for worship during the service. With our list of songs on a music stand before him, Dennis O'Dowd, whose turn it was to lead worship that day, was ready to begin.

Our pastor, Dave Harwood, wearily slung the bass guitar strap over his shoulder, then motioned for Dennis to wait. Dave looked tired and sick, but he began by encouraging the congregation to worship their God regardless of what had happened and how they felt. To proclaim to the heavens, to the earth, and to the devil himself that God was good and worthy of all praise.

Dave's exhortation struck a chord in me. The Bible was full of heartening people who had chosen to stand on God's side in the face of calamity and persecution. John the Baptist, Stephen, Job, King David, and Paul, to name just a few, were inspiring examples of faith and loyalty. I knew that I, too, needed to overcome, and now was as good a time as any to begin to practice what I had been preaching for the last twenty years.

Cindy, already with a resounding yes thundering within her heart, followed me up as I stood for the first song. At the moment, the only forgiveness I was concerned about was toward God. Others would have to be forgiven, too, but for now, first things were first.

Dennis began with a Hebraic song: "My lips shall sing the praises of the Lord, from this time forth and forever more." The chorus proclaimed, "You're my glory and the lifter of my head." My fists were clenched, and I tasted the salt from my tears as I sang out. When the song ended, Cindy began to openly and freely thank God for His mercy and faithfulness. I wasn't completely there yet in my heart or mind, but I was there in faith, so I joined in. The next song rang out with the same theme: "Let it ring from mountaintops and let my voice proclaim the tender mercies of the Lord . . .," and then a meditative rhythmic chant that repeats, "How I praise You. How I love You." These songs were derived from the Psalms, where God is worshiped amid all kinds of tragedies.

I am not so self-conscious that I always think everyone is watching me, but just then I knew that was the case. If we had sat there crushed under the weight of our loss, it would have been difficult, to say the least, for anyone in the congregation to enter into any form of corporate thanks and praise for all that God has done. But as I glanced around, I saw people worshiping wholeheartedly, hands raised to the sky and tears flowing. Cindy's hands were also raised, as was my right hand, the one she was holding.

The next song was bound to either make it or break it for me. A song I had written, derived from Psalm 148. A song that calls all—angels, peoples, nations, and all creation, even rain and fire—to praise God. Less than a year ago, beaming with enthusiasm, I had composed this song of praise. Now, I contrasted that time with this. I did not doubt God's existence; I simply wondered whether He was worthy of my praise. The fact that the entire congregation was singing as fervently as I'd ever heard it made little difference to me.

Cindy let go of my hand and bolted to the front of the room and started dancing. Several others joined her. I didn't know if I could worship that day from my heart, but after seeing the joyous praise of Cindy, who had lost both her daughter and her mother, I was determined to give it my best, which at the moment meant forcing any accusations against God out of my mind.

The very next song was another one I had written. It's a song that depicts God's control over everything that has happened since the beginning of time. As we sang the chorus, "You are Lord of all," I forced myself to confess this at the top of my lungs, with my clenched fists raised.

By the middle of the next song, most of the people were dancing, especially the children, many of whom were good friends with Robyn.

All of this may sound strange. However, worship, like love, is not always a feeling, but is always a decision. Sometimes the decision to worship God is harder to make than others, yet I have found that God provides enough grace to get me over any hump. Our worship lasted about ninety minutes, and then it was time for the pastor's message.

When I think of people who are spiritually impressionable and prophetically spontaneous, Pastor David Harwood is at the top of my list. In the twenty years I had heard him preach, he had done some pretty surprising things, most of which had been what I would call God-breathed and inspiring. On this day I would be surprised again and inspired.

Two minutes into his message, which focused on the absolute necessity of having the words of the Bible anchor your life, he steered his gaze from the general congregation and spoke directly to us, as if Cindy and I were the only people in the room. For the next half hour, his words pierced my heart. At a time when no one had anything to say but "I don't know what to say except that I'm sorry," Dave suddenly had a lot to say. His words were loving and exhorting at the same time, encouraging us to look to God for our strength. He emphasized that the Bible was full not just of words, but of promises, and then he cited a few.

He then turned his gaze to the rest of the congregation and spoke to them about us for the next half hour. For his text he used a verse whose first half probably rates as the most unpopular promise in the entire Bible: "In the world you will have tribulation" (John 16:33 NKJV). When it comes, Dave asked, what are you going to do with it? Follow the world's many philosophies and psychology, or follow God? One does not have to exclude the other, but it very often does. "But be of good cheer," said Jesus in the second half of the verse, "I have overcome the world."

CHAPTER 12

LAST JOURNAL ENTRIES

(CINDY)

Robyn began keeping her journal, as she had promised, the first afternoon of the trip:

Tuesday afternoon, June 25, 1996
Here I am, in Pennsylvania. I'm sorry I couldn't write when I was in New Jersey, but I couldn't find my notebook. Anyway, here in Pennsylvania, I really like the mountains and valleys.

Now it is about 2? hours later. We just got into Ohio and found an inn for the night.

Wednesday, June 26, 1996
Grandma, Grandpa, and I drove for about 1? hours before we got breakfast at Burger King. After I ate, I got this crazy new pen. It is about 10 in. long! It is also filled with liquid and sparkles. I'll come back to you when we reach a new state.

HI MOM! Guess what state I'm in? Yup. That's right, I'm in Indiana. The land out here is really flat! We still have a lot of driving to do. There are about seventy-seven more miles to travel till we're out of this state. The trees and farmland here are very nice.

Oh, I forgot to tell you that when we were in Ohio, I finished the *Princess Megan* book you gave me. It was really good.

Right now, I just came out of Illinois (I forgot to write). I also just passed over the Mississippi River.

It is now about fifteen minutes later. A little while ago, I came out of an Iowa visitor center. It was really interesting. There were maps and a little gift shop in it.

Thursday, June 27, 1996

Last night we found an inn that had an indoor pool. We were swimming in it past 10 P.M.! Right now I'm driving on the road (well, Grandpa's driving). All the farms are nice and clean—no garbage or anything. I'll write again soon.

I just got into Nebraska, and we have to drive three hundred eighteen more miles till I'm out of Nebraska. Isn't that a lot?! The time here is 1:27. That means it's 2:27 at home. I'll write again when something is interesting.

We just stopped at a motel for the night. Good thing it has an indoor pool!

Friday, June 28, 1996

Good morning, we're on the road. There are about six hundred thirty-seven miles to travel until we get to Aspen's house.

We just passed about four hundred animals. The car had the beautiful aroma of a farmyard.

CHAPTER 13

ROBYN'S BROTHERS AND SISTER

(BILL)

If bombs were dropping from the sky or if the house was burning down, we would know to gather our children and count heads. As it was, Cindy and I were so decapitated that we often did not know where our other children were, except that they were somewhere in our house or on our property with trusted friends. One or two of the kids were always visible, and the brief distraction of a hug or consolation was as much a help for me as for them.

Peter, six at the time of the crash, spent time sitting on the attic stairway, head in hands, rocking back and forth, praying, "Jesus bring me peace," over and over. Robyn was Peter's Pied Piper. He would follow her everywhere and enjoy her friendly, affectionate attention.

Willy, almost eight, was scared and confused from the very moment he saw Cindy running and screaming out the front door. The fact that he had lost a sister and a grandmother didn't really set in until he saw the caskets. *Wham*. The reality that had hit Cindy and me days before came crashing upon him. All the attention from family and friends that had detoured his focus with good food, candy, and soda (rare items in our home) could no longer cloud the facts.

Luke, nine, was away at camp when we found out. We were scared of how he would react because he and Robyn were very close and he was a sensitive guy. He knew something was odd when our friends picked him and his friend up from camp. His friend's parents were friendly, but not *this* friendly. When he got home he wondered why all the people were there. He appeared brave when he heard the news from Cindy and me who had gathered him up and sat alone with him on the couch in the den. He immediately tried to comfort us and himself by saying that they were now in heaven with Jesus. Then, almost unnoticed, he slipped away and went to Robyn's room where he could be alone with his tears and memories. He had often followed Robyn as she would take care of her many rabbits and guinea pigs, helping her wherever he could. He was there to carry food and help clean. At the funeral, he was a pallbearer for Robyn's pink casket. His final act of faithful service.

Stephen, a week from turning thirteen, was the first to hear the news, alone at home. My own distress over his condition caused me to race home through dozens of red lights. He was in deep pain and would take longer than the others to semi-recover, which is all any of us have managed. He loved his sister dearly and could often be found alone in tears in the following year. Once, months after the crash, I was disturbed from my bed hearing agonizing cries from his room. I rushed in. He had imagined that someday he might be an old man and having known Robyn for only eleven years, what would then be only a small percentage of his life, and might not remember her as well as he wanted to. I crawled onto his bed and cried with him. It was not the first time and it would not be the last.

Summer was almost four. Robyn had wanted one gift in life above all others; a baby sister. Both Robyn and Janice were there at Summer's birth in our bedroom. When Summer was born, Robyn treated her like a doll. The care and love shown to Summer will never be forgotten. Robyn was Summer's second mother and primary example. In everything she wanted to be like Robyn, and in many ways, still does. They were inseparable. Robyn read stories to her every day, slept by her side, changed her diapers, kissed her goodnight. Summer's memories of her big sister are vivid and she has no problem wearing her clothes and talking about her as if she is away on a trip. Robyn's name is on her lips nearly every day. Robyn's fruit shines through Summer's eyes.

CHAPTER 14

TO HELL WITH HATRED

(BILL)

The wait for the bodies to be processed and brought back from Nebraska to New York was grueling, but in truth, Cindy and I needed that time and more to prepare ourselves to see the coffins. To this day, I've been in the cemetery only once since the funeral, and that was for the burial of a close friend's wife. I can speak the words, "My daughter Robyn was killed," but I can't bear to see the gravesite. Nor could I at the wake, which began five days after the crash, deal with an open coffin. I couldn't bear to see her name attached to anything related to death, much less her lifeless body in a coffin.

I knew my daughter was with God, but the thought of her little body . . . well, my mind would rush to dwell some other place, which was difficult, since the usual concerns of the day held zero interest for me. The job, the bills, my health, the novels I was writing, food, baseball, the daily newspaper—I couldn't have cared less. Only one thing mattered. My precious daughter was dead. Never again would I see her dazzling smile, hear her pleading for the last mango. I would instantly trade anything to see Robyn one more time but not in a coffin.

Both Robyn and Jan were in the same room at the funeral home, a few feet apart. Janice's coffin was open. Robyn's casket was pink, her favorite color. Flowers were everywhere. I'm just beginning to like flowers again. For the last couple of years they have symbolized death instead of the sweeter part of life that they really are.

The first few days after the crash, I couldn't even look at a photo of Robyn. I was afraid to. Seeing her smile and bright eyes would break me to pieces. Slowly I allowed myself to look at one photo and then another until I was finally able to help put together a selection of photographs for the funeral. My father bought two sheets of four-by-four-foot Plexiglas, and we sandwiched dozens of pictures of Robyn between them. We then mounted the collage on an easel next to the casket.

I kept my favorite photo out of the mix and set it on the coffin. It was a picture of Robyn skating. In a white sweatshirt, white sweat-pants, white gloves, and white skates, she stood with her feet apart and her arms spread wide, hands and fingers stretching out from her sides as far as she could. Her long brown hair flowed over her shoulders, and her pretty face was deliriously happy, as if she were saying, "Tah-dahhhh! If only you could see me now."

The room, all the lounges, corridors, and doorways were full of people. A line of people waiting to get in went out the building and into the parking lot. Seeing so many people, and many of them for the first time in years, kept my mind busy. Kept me from thinking about the one thing I didn't want to think about: life without Robyn.

Herb Vanhooser, a longtime acquaintance for whom I had built a couple of Christian bookstores, embraced me, and then like everyone else, he told me that he was very sorry and that he didn't know what to say. And like everyone else, he took a short walk to the collage of photos. Then he said something that no one else had said. One word. One word that bore such witness in my spirit that all I could hear in my mind and heart was an emphatic *Yes!*

"Thief," Herb said thickly, shaking his head slowly, frowning in obvious anger, tears in his eyes.

Upon hearing the word *thief*, I immediately thought of a Scripture verse. Words spoken by Jesus, recorded in the gospel of John in the tenth verse of the tenth chapter: "The thief comes only to steal, and kill, and destroy; I came that they might have life, and might have it abundantly."

Herb was right. My family had been robbed of two precious lives. Robyn and Jan had been killed, and now, with pain and hatred and vengeance for his tools, the thief would work to destroy.

Thief.

Until Herb said that word, my anger had been spread around. I was angry with God, and my faith was tainted with doubt. I was angry with the drunken woman in Nebraska for being behind the wheel. I was angry with both my in-laws for taking Robyn on the trip, for being in the wrong place at the wrong time. And I was angry with myself for allowing Robyn to go on the trip, as though somehow by keeping her at home I could have kept her safe.

But when I heard the word *thief*, I suddenly felt I had been manipulated, like a brainless stringed puppet. Drugged with grief and despair, and blinded with rage, I had focused my anger in the wrong direction.

After Herb walked away, I continued to stare at the collage, his word echoing in my mind. He was right and I knew it. *I knew it.* The strange thing was that I had known it before Herb said anything, but his word ripped open the shutters and let in the light. Being mad at God had allowed darkness to shroud me. Everything I had been taught and had taught others about God's mercy, love, and forgiveness, I was keeping at arm's length. And that was exactly what the thief wanted.

Nothing is more important than my relationship with God and its continued growth. If I seek His kingdom, He promises to transform me into His image and likeness, but if I fall into the trap of wallowing in self-pity and bitterness against anyone, especially God, I'll cease to grow. That was exactly what the thief wanted. Instead of transforming into God's likeness, I'll be stuck for the rest of my life as a stagnant likeness of the thief who robbed me of my daughter.

Satan is a thief and a manipulator. He wants to take away what God gives, and he'll use anything he can to do it. He whispers accusations of polluted truth and points a finger, and he delights the most when fingers are pointing at everyone but him. Then destruction comes. Anger and bitterness consume all life.

Pain, suffering, and death were introduced to this world by a thief who thrives on the cycling and recycling of hatred, accusations, lies, and bitterness. In the book of Job, we can see how fast Satan is to accuse and how adept he is at suggesting and implementing calamity in its many forms.

Would I go to bed with the devil and perpetuate this cycle of bitterness by focusing my wrath on a woman running from her own pain, or my in-laws, who were only seeking their granddaughter's company and happiness, or myself, for not being a more protective father? *No! No! No!* If the devil was my real enemy—and he is—then I would not shoot at his targets. I would set my sights on him and forgive them all.

I had always considered the devil to be like a beehive. Don't bother the hive, and the hive won't bother you. I was wrong. Dead wrong. He comes after anyone and everyone.

Herb's word and these subsequent thoughts kept replaying in the back of my mind, even as I spoke with the people who continued to pour in and offer us their speechless condolences. Then Robyn's friend Tori handed me a letter she had written to Robyn and a neck-

This whole page is great

lace with both names engraved on it. She asked if the items could be placed in the casket. After asking Tori's permission, I read the letter. Once again, I was awash in grief and had to turn to Mark for help. He told me Tori's request was as good as done.

Cindy stood by the doorway, a pillar of strength. She was surrounded by her mother's friends, many of whom had known Cindy since she was a little girl. Every time I checked to be sure she was doing all right, Cindy seemed to be comforting the very ones who had come to comfort her.

Later, when visitation was over, Cindy said we needed to say good night to Jan and Robyn. I hadn't seen this coming, and I stood back, almost undone by her strength. Cindy first went to her mom, touched her hair and told her she loved her. "Oh, Mom," she said. "How I wish you were here. I need to talk to you."

Then she moved over to Robyn's pink casket. My heart was about to get another nail hammered into it. With her body draped over the casket, Cindy sang a lullaby that she used to sing to Robyn when she was a baby.

> Sleep sound in Jesus, my baby, my dear.
> Angels are watching, they keep you so near.
> Know for His sake you'll be safe for the night.
> Sleep sound in Jesus, I'll turn out the light.
>
> Sleep sound in Jesus, sweetheart of my heart.
> The dark of the night will not keep us apart.
> When I lay you down in your bed for the night,
> He holds you gently till morning is light.

CHAPTER 15

A FUNERAL AND A PROMISE

(BILL)

Friday morning, a week after the crash. The day of the funeral. By this time I had forgotten that there ever was another world or that I ever had another life that didn't include narrowly focused pain, grief, tears, consoling, and faith.

Cindy's four brothers struggled with their mother's casket up the steps of the Valley Stream Assembly of God Church, Jan's church. Assisted by three of my closest friends, I easily handled Robyn's casket. It was very light. In fact, its lightness made it harder for me to carry, reminding me again that my little girl was inside. This would be the last time I would carry her. Memories of all the rides I had given her on my shoulders, spinning her slight body over my head, were now pummeling my heart. Indeed, the coffin was mercilessly light.

Inside the sizable church sanctuary, there was standing room only and not much of that. We placed the coffins next to each other in the center of the middle aisle and took our seats. After a brief word by Jan's pastor, Dave Harwood and I sang two songs. The first was one that I had written. I was fighting mad about what had happened, but I knew my fight was not with flesh and blood, and I wanted all to know where I stood and how big the hand was that was holding me up.

Emptiness, shapelessness, darkness over deep,
Your Spirit moved across the dark, a world half-made lay asleep.
Your presence and Your purpose there, desire met with might;
A want came through Your holy mouth, and there was light!
Awake, O world, the word of God commands you.
For the sake of the name above every name, we bow too;
You are Lord of all.
Bethlehem, Word made flesh, a King's born in a cave;
Prince of peace, Bread of Life, a world He came to save.
Mocked and scorned, crucified, thorns placed in His head;
Empty tomb, an angel cries, "He's risen from the dead!"
Worthy, worthy is the Lamb of God,
Who was and is and is to come;
You are Lord of all.
Battles rage, lies sound true, the love of most grows cold;
Saints are slain, the gospel's preached, everywhere so bold.
Israel cries, "Messiah, come!" The fig tree sprouts its leaves;
The sky rolls back, a blinding light, the world's down on its knees.
Arise and shine, for Your light has come;
From New Jerusalem, the wedding feast has begun,
And You are Lord of all.

After we sang, Robyn's girlfriends did a dance in memory of her and in praise to God. Robyn had danced with the girls every week, and it was nearly impossible for me to watch them without her being among them or to think of watching them grow older without her. I tried to imagine Robyn dancing in heaven, now praising God in His very presence.

Finally, Cindy walked up and stood behind the pulpit. I had no idea what she was going to say, but she had told us earlier that she wanted to speak at the funeral. Before she got up, I asked her if she was sure she wanted to do this. I was so afraid she was going to fall apart up there. "I have to," she said. So I sat there and prayed that God would give her strength.

And He did.

She did a great job. She spoke confidently and boldly about Robyn and her mom and about their faith. Afterward, one woman told me that Cindy's message held everyone together. The message was taped, and for the next two months we had many requests for copies to help other friends and families who had lost loved ones.

• • •

(CINDY)

Over the preceding week, it had become clear to us that Robyn's gentle, caring spirit had found its way into the hearts of many of her friends. We knew how close she was to some of the girls, but we were surprised—and yet not surprised—to learn that many of her girlfriends considered Robyn to be their *best* friend. And it wasn't just the emotion of the moment speaking. They would back up their declaration by relating specific times when Robyn had reached out to them in love and friendship. She had an eye for those who were on the periphery, and she would seek to include them in her circle.

Several people spoke that morning, and Lauren Eskenazi, Mark and Linda's daughter, read a poem she had written for her friend.

ROBYN'S SONG
Dedicated to Robyn Snow Griffiths, a great friend

Robyn Snow Griffiths cared for everyone,
She was always building up, and had lots of fun.
She was a sister to all, and a daughter to some,
But poor Robyn did not know what was to come.
June 28th, '96,
She died in a car accident that no one could fix.
Well Robyn is dead now, and that is not good,
We all tried to love her as well as we could.
Robyn is gone, apart from me and you,
I loved her so, everyone else did too.
While my heart is broken and torn into shreds,
I will cherish all the good things that she said.
Although thoughts and memories seem like they faded away,
They are in my heart, forever to stay.
From my heart comes a terrible groan,
But I know the Truth,
She's standing in sight of the Throne.

We played Robyn's favorite music, including "Für Elise," the piano piece she had been learning but never got to finish, and a song we had heard her singing often in the last month or so, Amy Grant's "Straight Ahead." I can't describe the emotions I would go through, remembering my little girl singing this precious song of life, faith, and determination to march straight ahead after God, through whatever darkness until finally being with God Himself.

Then Robyn's friends danced to "All Your Promises Are True." Bill and I first heard the song in Mark's car the day we were picking the cemetery. In our church, various expressions of worship are encouraged, including dance. Scripture says, "Let them praise His name with dancing" (Ps. 149:3). Usually during a worship service, the children will follow an adult leader and dance and skip around in praise of God. Robyn loved to do this.

My friend Lois Pena, a member of our church dance group, put together a dance for the funeral. The young girls waved colored scarves and danced as joyfully as they could. I wondered whether Robyn and my mom were watching.

Then it was my turn. As difficult as I knew it would be, I also knew that I had to speak. And although in times past I had been self-conscious about public speaking, that morning I didn't worry about saying the right things. I didn't care. Something bigger than being afraid to talk to a group of people had happened. I had no way of knowing that the boldness I experienced that morning was going to be a part of my life in the days ahead.

As I spoke, I found myself being filled with words about God, the Promise Keeper. How He was with me, comforting me. How He would be faithful to cause the tragedy to be used for good in the future. And how He would keep His promises of eternal life to those who love Him.

• • •

(BILL)

Two hours later we were all at the cemetery, its small rolling hills and valley paths filled with people. My mind still reverberated with the revelation of the "thief" I'd had two days earlier. I felt God had made me a promise, and I shared it with those gathered at the gravesite: "According to my belief, we are in an age of death, but it was not intended to be that way in the beginning. The evil one is now having his turn, and his crimes against God are mounting and have been mounting for a long time. Every crime, every spilled drop of blood, every tear, and every lost soul adds to a giant scale. At a precise time, the scale will tip. Then it will be God's turn. And I look forward to that day."

• • •

(CINDY)

While God had given me strength to speak the words He had given me at Robyn's funeral, at the burial I leaned on Bill the whole time. I don't think I could have stood under my own power. I remember seeing my boys on the opposite side of the grave from Bill and me. I wanted them next to us, but I was paralyzed with the reality of what we were doing there. Mom's casket was laid to rest first, with Robyn's on top.

Afterward, our neighbors Drew and Eileen Small and Drew's mother, Kay, served lunch at our neighborhood firehouse (Drew's a fireman). Many came there from the funeral, and once again we were blessed by our friends' love and kindness—gifts we will hold forever in our hearts.

Then the week was over. We had climbed an enormous mountain of terror and dread. We had trod an unhewn, unmerciful path that tore our hearts to shreds.

Now, somehow, we had reached a summit, and in the presence of these dear friends and family members, I felt a bit lighter. Yet I knew that this was but the first of a whole mountain range of peaks we would need to conquer in the days ahead.

PART 3

THE WAY

CHAPTER 16

DETOUR OF DEATH

(BILL)

One night, soon after the funeral, I found myself in another manic conversation with God. Mercifully, God seemed to allow me angry outbursts in my spirit while trying to gain understanding from Him. As angry as I would get, He would never walk away from His side of our conversation as long as I was willing to stay.

"Why is death part of life's equation?" I asked, searching, as if there were an answer that could somehow bring Robyn back. In my mind I saw death everywhere. I remembered reading a newspaper trivia clip that lists famous people's birthdays under "Born Today," most of them long dead, the rest soon to be. I recalled the same paper once told me that the population of the world is still exploding with more people being born than dying every day. The numbers were staggering. I began to see all the births as deaths and then wondered how many people have ever died.

I picked up a Bible and began reading at the beginning. Soon I was reading verses dealing with the tree of the knowledge of good and evil, and I stayed there for a while. Clearly, this tree or whatever it symbolized turned out to be the beginning of the end for Adam and Eve and the rest of the world who followed them. "Of every tree of the garden you may freely eat; but of the tree of the knowledge of good and evil you shall not eat, for in the day that you eat of it you shall surely die" (Gen. 2:16–17 NKJV).

The knowledge of good and evil or, as both God and Satan refer to it in later verses, "Knowing good and evil." I wondered, *What's wrong with knowing about good and evil?* It would seem to me that such knowledge would be important, to say the least. I teach my children the difference between right and wrong, not only so they mature morally but also so they hopefully don't get themselves killed in the process. Why would God not want His young creation to know what to do and what not to do? And why couldn't man figure this stuff out without eating it from a tree?

As I searched, a concept I had never considered occurred to me. I had always seen the emphasis being on the words *good* and *evil*. Now, however, I began to focus on the word *know*. Taking in "know" within the context of "you shall surely die" changed my entire interpretation of the verse and it also changed my perspective on death. "You shall surely die" was a promise, not one of God's more popular promises, like, "Delight yourself in the Lord and He will give you the desires of your heart," or, "He who calls on the name of the Lord shall be saved," but a promise nonetheless and one I have automatically inherited.

Whether because of my interest in human origins, or because I've always believed real science is a study of God and, therefore, the two should be in closer harmony than either fundamental Christianity or modern science seem willing to allow themselves to admit, I've enthusiastically studied both theistic evolution and creationism, and much that falls in-between. I've read everything I could find on the first three chapters of Genesis, which deal with creation and the fall of man. The tree of the knowledge of good and evil, in particular, has always held a mysterious curiosity for me. But every commentary on God's warning about "the knowledge of good and evil" I found to be academic—the most common interpretation being that God decided that man wasn't able to handle such knowledge.

That night, however, I was compelled by something very different. I was hearing "know" the way a man *knows* fear because a grizzly bear just stepped in front of him, and the way he *knows* pain because the bear just sank its teeth and claws into his flesh. The way a woman *knows* pain when giving birth. The way parents *know* hate when their daughter has been raped and strangled. And the way my wife and I *know* grief and sorrow because our daughter and mother were killed in a senseless car accident.

Know. Not, know about. *Know.* Experiential, not academic.

As if God, in judgment for Adam and Eve's sin of disobedience, said, "So, you want to know good and evil? Okay . . . *know it!*"

Think of trying to explain anger to someone who has never been angry. Imagine trying to explain pain to someone who has never been hurt. Besides the fact that you would probably have to go to another planet in search of such a student, your lesson would be a failure until you finally slapped him or her hard in the face a few times.

That night, I no longer saw the tree of the knowledge of good and evil as a tree, alive with broad limbs and green leaves. Instead, I saw the embodiment of a life, a life that would spread upward and outward through generational branches. A life full of consequences. The tree represented a choice that God had given to His creation, yet fervently wanted man to stay clear of.

Angrily, I asked, "Why put the tree there in the first place? Why

allow Your creation even the remotest chance of making such a dis-
astrous choice?"

I knew the first half of the answer even as I was asking the question. As a new believer I was taught that God does not want robots;
He wants a two-way love relationship with His creation. That was
why He created us in the first place. But for men or women to choose
love, they must have the free will to choose hate. A robot could be
programmed to respond correctly in every instance, but a mutual
growing relationship with a robot is impossible. For a relationship
built on positive responses to be meaningful, there must be an option
for negative responses. Unless we can make the choice to shun hate,
the deciding act is devoid of life.

The second half of the answer is what stood out and caused me to
remember this night. As usual, I did not hear an audible voice or even
an internal one. But I suddenly found myself earnestly considering the
extreme detail Moses took in describing the tabernacle, the ark of the
covenant, various altars and clothing, and even the dimensions of
Noah's ark. Then my focus shifted to the infamous tree first introduced in Genesis 2. The tree of the knowledge of good and evil.

No doubt Moses could have been hyper-focused when it came to
revealing particulars. Did he spare one stroke of his pen when he
delineated the law and its consequences? Yet strangely, when it came
to this tree with the poisonous fruit, which has affected mankind
more than anything else in God's creation, he doesn't describe it at
all. Nothing! No size, shape, color, scent, texture, foliage—not even
the slightest hint of its surroundings. That night, I firmly believed I
understood why.

The tree of the knowledge of good and evil was suddenly no
more a tree to me than Jesus was a door, vine, root, stone, lamb, or
bread. I was no longer stuck on seeing this as a literal tree. This tree

was like no other in that it housed God's response to a choice man had to be allowed to make.

I remembered how sly the serpent was in telling Eve that the tree would make her like God. A crafty mixture of truth and lie. How easy it was for him. A promise that Adam and Eve could decide their own rules and regulations. They could take what they wanted when they wanted it. And the big one—the right to claim full credit and recognition for their accomplishments. All this beauty was pleasing to Eve's eyes and exciting for her future, and the tempter told her that the decision to eat would also make her wise.

The problem was that in order to have all this, she and Adam had to place their faith on their own shoulders. In other words, they had to remove the faith they had in the Creator—the One who had given them their very life and provided for their every need—and place their faith on a far lesser god: self.

Of course, the all-knowing, all-seeing God heard the infamous conversation that Eve had with the serpent, whether it was Lucifer himself or one of his underlings. How the heart of God must have broken to see His beloved children conversing with His enemy and believing his lies. But He would not stop it. He had to allow free will to operate. He had to allow them to choose.

God had given them clear warning. "The day that you eat from [the tree]"—the day you choose to serve another god—"you shall surely die" (Gen. 2:17).

Well, we know what their choice was, and now nobody gets out of here alive. *Nobody.*

"You shall *know* good and evil." The promise was a curse. The fruit Adam and Eve ate was the fruit of selfish ambition, pride, and the determination to be in charge of themselves. From what I was seeing, the devil's task was an easy one. Even as I write this, I remember Al

Pacino playing Satan in *The Devil's Advocate* saying with a smile, "Vanity . . . definitely my favorite sin." How accurate. All the serpent had to do was to get Adam and Eve's eyes on themselves. They chose to be gods, and the fruit they ate was death. How painful it must have been for God to have watched this happen. No wonder the first commandment declares that He alone is God and that other gods will not be tolerated.

That night, my angry question was answered. So *this* was why death was part of life's equation. My tears of anger turned to tears of thanksgiving as I suddenly realized that in God's infinite foresight and love and mercy, He included another piece to the equation. There was something else hidden inside the tree. Inside was a merciful antidote. A way out. The opportunity to make another choice. Not only would His creation know evil, but it would also know good. Just as He knew mankind would make the decision they did, God also knew that He would bail us out. He didn't owe us that. We walked away from God. But God is love—and the only way to redeem the sin committed was to redeem it Himself, through the death of His Son on the cross.

That night I found a renewed peace, reinforced in the faith that death is just a detour on the infinite highway of God's eternal purposes.

CHAPTER 17

ENCOUNTERING SALT

(BILL)

Ultimately the controversial decisions we have made since June 1996 were born from decisions Cindy and I made, separately but coincidentally, in 1977. It was then that I came upon a fork in life's road and went in the direction that made possible the decision to forgive Verma Harrison. I firmly believe that if I had stayed on the path I was on, forgiveness would never have entered my mind. Any decision would have been born from death and eventually produced death.

Life was quite comfortable, convenient, and enjoyable in 1977, and then without any warning, God wrecked it.

A couple of years earlier, in 1975 and at twenty years of age, I had a goal of opening a nightspot where young people could gather, listen to good live music, dance, and drink. I intended to call it The Party. Everyone always wanted to know where the party was, so I thought I'd provide an address. I wouldn't serve alcohol. Not that I had anything against drinking—quite the contrary. But buying drinks at the

bar was expensive for my local Long Island friends who were still trying to figure out what they were going to do with their lives. To save
money at my place, they could bring their own beer and liquor. I
would collect a reasonable fee at the door and supply soft drink vend-
ing machines so my patrons could mix their own drinks.

As a self-employed carpenter, painter, and handyman working with
friends, I saved whatever money I could toward my goal. To further
economize, I decided to make my own tables for The Party. In fact, I
became obsessed with the idea—all I could think about was tables.
They had to be big, they had to be strong, and they had to be unique.

One Sunday, while walking through the Museum of Natural
History in Manhattan with a couple of friends, thinking about nothing
but tables as we toured *T. rex* skeletons and evolutionary charts, I turned
a corner and saw a crosscut slice from a giant sequoia tree. It was
twenty-five feet in diameter and had little white historical trivia cards
attached to a number of its annual rings. My friends entertained themselves reading the dated cards that indicated how big the tree was
when George Washington crossed the Delaware, and when Columbus
discovered America, and when Attila the Hun was invading Roman
civilization. Meanwhile, all I saw was a fantastic model of a tabletop.

Freshly inspired, I bought a chainsaw and began slicing up fat
trees wherever I could find them. I would remove trees for free as
long as I could slice them up where they fell. But early on in my
industrious endeavor, something unexpected happened. People
wanted to buy my tree slices. Lots of people. *Sure, why not?* I thought.
At fifty bucks a slice, I'd be able to put my bar business together all
the sooner. One guy even let me cut down his five-foot-diameter
maple for free, then bought back half the slices for family and friends.

Some of the slices made it back to my father's garage, where I
sanded them down and fitted them with legs that I also fashioned

from the tree. My new bar tables drew even more attention and customers. To improve the look, I teamed up with a friend who finished surfboards and bar tops with a clear resin, and a girlfriend whose artistic touch provided pen-and-ink mountain, jungle, and wildlife scenes. The tables were supposed to attract attention to my club, not to themselves, but before long I became so focused on the tables and the surprise business surrounding them that I lost my enthusiasm for The Party. I decided I would ride the table thing out for all it was worth. If the tables were only a fad, I could always develop the social club concept later.

That winter we found ourselves at the New York Coliseum International Craft Show. By then, our inventory also included clocks, pen holders, and mirrors, all made from tree sections of every size. The show was a success for us, leaving many potential customers asking one question: "Where's your showroom?"

I couldn't very well give them directions to my father's garage. I needed a location. Great Neck, a local affluent town with a good flow of walking traffic, became my first choice. I advertised for a shared situation or a back alley fixer-upper. The day the paper came out I got my first and only response. A Great Neck proprietor owned an old barn in need of extensive repair in Glen Cove, a nearby town on Long Island's north shore. Glen Cove wasn't quite the walking town Great Neck was, but I needed an address, and I felt sure that people would travel once they knew where to travel to. Besides, I liked the back alley location off the main street and a few stores down from the north shore's only dinner playhouse. After a little friendly negotiating with the owner, we agreed that I would rebuild the barn in exchange for two years of free rent.

I couldn't have been more excited. I had money in my pocket and would soon be opening a new business; I had many friends and no enemies; and I had a rich relationship with a great girl. My only problem was finding enough time to hang out and party. Life was great.

My best friend, Rich Ortner, whom I had known most of my life, went with me to New Hampshire to purchase rough white pine planks from a sawmill. The two-foot-wide virgin planks would be perfect for the warm, rustic feel I wanted to create in the barn as a backdrop for my tables. And buying directly from the mill, I was guaranteed the best wood at the best price.

I returned from New Hampshire with more than enough white pine to accomplish all that I needed. The next morning, I showed up at the barn, ready both mentally and physically to work. I strapped on my tool belt, slipped my hammer into its holster, filled my pouches full of 8D and 10D galvanized nails, slipped a pencil over my right ear, laid the circular saw on the ground next to the wood pile, and unraveled a new one-hundred-foot yellow extension cord to plug into the one outlet that my landlord had designated for my use at a neighboring building on the same property. That's when I ran into a small technical problem. The outlet was very old and didn't have a ground slot for my modern plug. I searched my toolbox for a three-prong adapter, but couldn't find one. I was ready to do the wrong thing and rip the ground prong off my cord when I saw a man, also wearing a tool belt, come out of a back door, not thirty feet away. He walked to an old pickup, where he seemed to be looking for something.

"Excuse me," I said, walking toward him, dragging my extension cord by the plug.

The man turned. He was about thirty, and his light blond hair and eyebrows and bright blue eyes were almost startling. He smiled peacefully, and if his eyes hadn't been so clear and wide open, the smile would have made me think he was stoned.

"You, uh, wouldn't happen to have a three-prong adapter?" I said, holding the cord up like a little flag.

He frowned thoughtfully and said, "I've only got the one I'm using." Then the smile returned. "But you can use that one. I'll just use another cord with a broken-off tip," he said as he walked past me.

"Hey, thanks, but don't worry about it. I'll just break off this tip," I called as I watched him disappear into the door.

Moments later, he reappeared. "My name's Bill," I said warmly as he handed me the small gray adapter.

"And I'm Tom," he said. "It looks like you've got quite a project on your hands."

"Yeah," I agreed, glancing over my left shoulder. "And this is day one."

He nodded. "Me too," he said.

Anxious to get to work, I didn't want to get delayed by chitchat about our respective projects. I could always talk to him later while taking a break. "Well, I best get to work, Tom. Thanks," I said, holding up the adapter and turning to leave.

"Thank the Lord, Bill," he said.

I acknowledged him with a casual nod and a wave as I walked away, but my reaction was a lie. I was twenty-two years old, and nobody had ever casually told me to thank the Lord. For what? Thank the Lord that the guy had a three-prong adapter so I wouldn't have to break off the ground plug on my own extension cord? *I might as well just thank the Lord for everything if I'm going to do that,* I thought. I could just imagine some little kid dogging my heels, thanking me for my shadow. Before long I'd wind up telling the kid to shut up and get lost. God would likely do the same. Uh-uh, no thanks. I was an agnostic. My conversations with the Lord would be rare and valuable and saved for something important.

When it was time to take a lunch break, I stayed out of sight. Generally I was a people person and enjoyed company, but I didn't enjoy bizarre conversation with sincere people—especially sincere religious people. My little world was moving along just fine. Nor did spiritual thoughts enter my world. God had His busy schedule and I had mine. His was hectic enough with important stuff, like world hunger. Just suppose I gained His attention with some little thing and He didn't like the way I led my life? From what I'd been taught in eight years of Catholic school, the Lord might be forgiving, but He would probably not approve of my anything-but-puritanical social life.

The next day my partner, Ron, who specialized in finishing the tables, came out to the barn to help. When I told him about our neighbor Tom and the "thank the Lord" comment, he rolled his eyes. "Great!" he said sarcastically.

While we were working, Tom waved to us. Today, there was another man with him, mid-forties and casually dressed, but not in work clothes.

"Greetings," the older man called out.

I waved back, hammer in hand.

"What are you building?" he called.

"A woodworking shop," Ron answered.

"Excellent!" he said, walking toward us, leaving Tom to continue his work. "I'm Mike, your new neighbor."

I looked at Ron and holstered my hammer, then turned to meet my new neighbor.

"We're opening a Christian bookstore. I see you're getting your electricity from our building. Do you have any running water or plumbing yet?" he asked.

"Uh, no," I admitted. "We've been using the diner up the block when we need to."

"Well, you can use ours, too, if you like. Our water is your water, as are our bathroom and air-conditioning. Anytime you men want to come in and cool off, I want you to feel completely free to do so."

"That's very generous of you, Mike. Thanks. I'm Bill, and this is my partner, Ron," I said, fully expecting him to tell me to thank the Lord. He didn't. But what he did tell me made me wish for a simple "thank the Lord."

"Do you know the Lord?" he asked, looking at me.

At first I stared blankly at him. In my entire religious upbringing in Saint Aidan's School, I had never been asked this question, nor had I ever heard it asked of anyone else.

After a long, awkward moment, I smiled and looked at Ron, hoping that between the two of us we could lighten up the conversation.

"Know the Lord? Me? Do you mean, do I believe there's a God?"

"No, that's not what I mean. But *do you* believe there's a God?"

"Maybe sometimes. To tell you the truth, I haven't thought about it that much in the last ten years," I said. *Not since the last time I got beaten up by a Franciscan brother,* I thought. *Not since I got out of parochial school.*

"How about you, Ron?" he said, turning to my partner. "Do you know the Lord?"

"I guess I believe there's a God, but not as much as I did when I was a kid," Ron said. "It's been a while since I've been to church."

The most spiritual thing Ron and I had ever talked about was whether or not fortune cookies were more or less reliable than newspaper horoscopes. We didn't know the answer to *that* either.

"It sounds like you both need to be saved!" Mike said unabashed, and he wasn't smiling.

"Saved?" I said. "From what?"

"Hell. If you die without knowing the Lord, you go to hell," he said. *Obviously this guy wasn't interested in pulling any punches for the sake of first impressions. Doesn't he know he's making a fool of himself?* I thought. *Doesn't he care? Hey, how ya doin'? My name's Mike and I'm your new neighbor. What's mine is yours, help yourself to anything and everything, and oh, by the way, you're goin' to hell.*

Then came a scary thought. If this guy, Mike, was brazen enough to deliver his gloomy message to me, he might very well be fanatical enough to deliver it to my clientele. Why not? I could picture him saying, "Excuse me," to people who were just about to enter my showroom, then pleasantly tell them that they were going to hell.

Yet there was something about his boldness that struck a chord in my confrontational makeup. "Do you ask everyone you don't know if he knows the Lord?" I said.

"Everyone the Lord tells me to."

"You hear God speak to you?" said Ron.

"Yes. All the time," Mike replied matter-of-factly.

We're dead, I thought. *He hears voices, and then he acts on them. He's going to tell Ron and me every day that we're going to hell. "The voice" will remind him every time he sees us.*

The man didn't look as if he would hurt a fly, and I'm sure he would have more of a problem with my lifestyle than I would have with his. But the truth was, I wanted to start a new name for myself and for my business in this new location, and I didn't want my personal beliefs or any of my customers' beliefs threatened in the process.

"Look, Mike. This is the kind of conversation that could go on all day, and we both have a lot of work to do," I said, then motioned to Ron for us to get back to work. "It's been nice meeting you, and we'll talk again when we both have more time."

"Lord willing," Mike said as we were leaving.

"Excuse me?" I said.

"I said 'Lord willing.' There are no guarantees that God will grant us another meeting. This could be the last day for one or both of us. There are no guarantees. Lord willing, we'll be allowed to continue."

Great. The .01 percent of me that could possibly believe that what this man had to say might be true was surprisingly concerned at the urgency Mike portrayed. Why was he saying this to me? Why was he doing this to me? Did he think God was going to give him a commission for my soul? People who have known me my whole life wouldn't speak to me this way, even if they thought I *was* going to hell. And the probability was pretty good that some of them *did* think that. Who was he to be so intrusive?

"Who are you, anyway?" I said, annoyed and caring less by the second about being a good neighbor.

"Me?" he said, pointing at his chest. "I'm nobody. Nothing more than a servant spreading seeds. A salt shaker for God. I'm just a simple Jew who's grateful for God's mercy on my life."

If he is God's salt shaker, then the cap must have fallen off while I was getting sprinkled, I thought. All I wanted to do was rinse my mouth and spit.

"You're Jewish?" Ron asked.

"Yes."

"You believe in Jesus?" Ron asked.

"Yes."

"How can you be Jewish and believe in Jesus?" I was totally confused. I didn't understand what it meant to be a Christian, much less a Jewish Christian.

He laughed. "Jesus was Jewish . . . and so were most of the apostles."

"But that was then," I blurted.

"God hasn't changed His mind," Mike said.

. . .

Over the next twelve days, a heat wave pounded Long Island. Daytime temperatures hovered around 104, and the high humidity made it feel worse. During that time, Mike faithfully left his air-conditioned store at least twice a day to remind Ron and me of our perilous position and what we needed to do to change our fate.

I soon found myself hating the heat, hating the salty sweat dripping into my eyes, and most of all, hating Mike. He had me thinking about frightening prospects I didn't want to consider. He had cursed me with his redundant warnings of doom and allegories of life. His parabolic tidbits were now playing like annoying soda jingles in the back of my mind day and night. And I hated how relentlessly nice he was. I felt like smacking him in the face and telling him to get lost— except he'd probably just thank God for the privilege of suffering pain and humiliation as His servant.

Between the heat and Mike, my patience had worn paper thin. I was argumentative with everyone and having a hard time focusing on our project. With the twelfth day of record heat upon us, I'd finally had enough. I had just sat down with my usual lunch of two sandwiches, potato salad, and a quart of milk when I decided I wanted air-conditioning more than anything else in the world.

"Look, Ron," I said, putting my sandwich back in the bag. "We're going to get out of this steam bath and eat our lunch in that air-conditioned bookstore of his. He's going to welcome us with open arms and a twinkle in his eye and once again tell us to make ourselves at home. Then we're going to eat and breathe in cool seventy-degree air. And when he starts in about God, the devil, and the end of the world, we'll smile, nod, and keep eating and breathing in that cool air. We'll simply agree with everything he says. We'll nod him to death. Eventually he might even feel he's gotten through to us and leave us alone."

Ron was delirious from the heat, and anything that promised relief, however brief, was going to get his vote.

As expected, Mike was a living welcome mat. He unfolded a couple of metal chairs and stacked up a couple of cardboard boxes for a table.

"Can I get you some water?"

"No thanks, Mike. We're set," I said with my mouth full, holding up my quart of milk.

"Napkins?"

"We've got them," Ron said.

"If you need the bathroom, you know where it is."

We both nodded, munching away.

"So then," he said, rubbing his hands together.

Here it comes, I thought. *We must look to him like a turkey dinner on Thanksgiving Day, hot and ready to get devoured. He's licking his chops and thinks he'll eat us alive.*

"Did you ever think that it might be God turning up the heat on the whole East Coast just because He loves you and wants you to hear His word?"

Ron and I looked at each other, and then, as if on cue, we shrugged our shoulders in unison and nodded agreement to what may have been the most preposterous thing either of us had ever, *ever* heard.

For at least the next half hour, Mike continued to talk, and we continued to nod. We also learned some interesting things about our neighbor. We found out that Mike was an extremely successful businessman who had owned a seat on the New York Stock Exchange. To our surprise, he also confessed that he had not always been an honorable character but had committed some crimes. Then after becoming a believer, a story in itself, he left the financial world to study the Bible and spread what he called "the good news that saved my life."

Poor Mike, I thought. *He could be enjoying his millions on some beach in the Caribbean, but instead he feels compelled to open a Christian bookstore and talk to a couple of dirty, sweaty nobodies about God. Glad I'm not him.*

I was no longer hot. In fact, I was downright comfortable, except for one thing. It was becoming increasingly harder to agree with Mike. Being cool, I no longer felt such a desperate need to nod. His words, which had floated past me like bubbles earlier, were now sharp and piercing. Finally I could no longer nod like a bobble-head doll.

"What about the Hindus and the Buddhists? They don't curse, they don't fight, they don't kill, and they don't steal. All they do is pray and sit cross-legged until their eyes flutter. What's so wrong with them that they should be sent to hell? If they're not good enough for God, how could I ever be?"

"God is not a principle or a lifestyle. Salvation has no more to do with religious routine than marriage has to do with how you dress for the wedding. There is one God, and He extends His hand to all. He wants a living, growing relationship, not repetitious ritual. He wants to covenant with us. Would you want to marry someone who didn't want a growing relationship with you?"

"God wants to marry me?"

"Yes, in a way. We are spoken of as being His bride. Marriage is an institution from God and a foreshadow of a spiritual reality."

"And if you don't take God's hand in marriage, you go to hell? How do you know that God doesn't just send you somewhere else? Why does it always have to be hell with you?"

"What *is* hell?" Mike asked. "You think hell is a town filled with campfires where you hang out with all your friends, who, like you, didn't make it as angels? No! Hell is absolute, total separation from

God. The saying 'life is hell' is pathetically bogus and misleading. Despite all the horrors this world has to offer, God and His attributes are everywhere we look.

"Hell is all about what's not there," Mike continued. "God's not there. Love, light, interaction with others, peace, joy, warmth, and enthusiasm are just a few of the many attributes that come directly from God that are completely absent in hell. Hell is spoken of as being a place of outer darkness, where there is absolutely no light whatsoever. Love is at best, or should I say at worst, a memory. No love or anything that even resembles love. You are completely alone except for the demonic tormentors who thrive on pain and fear. Like there are billions of stars in the sky that are light-years apart, so you will be in hell, without any communion with anyone else. And you won't be able to escape even by going to sleep or getting drunk. The warmth of God won't be there in that cold, cold place."

Ron and I had stopped eating. For the first time Mike had our undivided attention. Neither of us had ever heard anything like it before, and true or not, it was captivating.

"And you know what's worse?" Mike said.

Worse?

"What's worse is that you're sent there by God Himself."

We frowned.

"Don't you understand? Think about it! You have to go to heaven to be sent to hell. Before you experience hell, you experience God and heaven. You're going to know what you're missing. That's why you hear about those near-death experiences of people walking through some tunnel of light before they come back to life. If they were to die and continue on that journey, they would travel through heaven, a place of unimaginable beauty and joy. With each step the realization becomes more and more intense, knowing that you belong there, created for this very place. And never is that knowledge more certain than when you arrive at the throne of God.

"Upon seeing God, you know with every essence of your being that this is your Father and that this is your home. You are drawn to Him completely as you bow to worship Him, as everyone else there is doing. It's the only appropriate response, now knowing that your true Father is the Almighty and deserves the worship of every created thing. You want nothing more than to be one with Him for all eternity, and all you can imagine is being completely soaked in His presence.

"You crave to remain in His presence forever . . . His presence . . . His presence . . . more . . . more . . . more. But just because you get to see Jesus and stand before the throne of God doesn't mean that you can dwell there. Everyone who goes to hell gets to see God in His magnificent glory, but then in final judgment you are told that you have to leave forever, to be with the god you chose to serve when you had a chance to choose. Yourself."

I had never heard anything like what he was saying in my life, and I hoped I never would again. The remote possibility that what this guy was saying was true was chilling, to say the least. There had to be some way to check this out. If I were to die and any of what he said was true, I would ricochet through heaven and go to hell. At that point, it wasn't the air-conditioning that made me shiver.

"Oh, I almost forgot," Mike said.

I wanted to cover my ears.

"There is an activity spoken of that takes place in hell. Weeping and gnashing of teeth. Weeping because now you've seen God and you know what you're missing, and gnashing your teeth in frustration because your state is eternal. Alone, alone, alone . . . forever and ever. You won't even think about what you're missing on earth after you've seen how great heaven and God are."

If he says one more thing about hell, I'm going to run out of here screaming, I thought.

"But what if you're a really good person?" Ron asked.

"Good is a myth," Mike answered. "Salvation is not about being good. It's about being God's."

"Wait a minute," I said. "What if Hitler confessed his sins and asked God for forgiveness just before he died? Would he go to heaven?"

"Yes."

"That's crazy!" I wanted all of this to be crazy. *Please, God, let it all be crazy. Let it be . . . wait . . . now who am I talking to?*

"None of us make it to heaven without taking our lives out of our own hands and placing them in His. The decision has to be ours."

"Can't you wait until you're old and then decide on your deathbed?"

"You'd be missing out on a lot. Eternal life begins when you make Jesus your life's source, not when you die. Besides, you might not have the convenience of dying in your bed."

Ron frowned. "If I ask God to save me, do I have to give up—"

Mike held up his hand like a traffic cop, stopping Ron in mid-sentence. "Go to the living God and ask Him whatever you want. He'll tell you His will concerning you. Whatever you give to God, He'll give you back a hundred times over. He's not looking to take away any good thing. He's looking to give. It's just that we need to have faith because we don't always know what's good or harmful."

Just so we knew that we weren't hearing the gospel according to Mike, he continually flipped through the pages of his Bible and let us read verses for ourselves. Most of the answers led to more questions, which led to more answers, and so on.

"Okay, okay," I said. "Granted, this book's got a lot of answers. But how do I know they're the right answers? How do I know these aren't answers developed by a bunch of guys who got a little carried away two thousand years ago? How do I know this is the truth? I happen to like my life just the way it is, and I don't like the life you're talking about . . . at all. Why should I change, when for all I know this might not even be true? I need proof. If God is as understanding as you say He is, He should be able to understand that."

"Proof?" said Mike. "What do you want, scientific proof, mathematical proof?"

"That would be nice."

"Okay, let's start with the math," he said confidently. He opened a cardboard box that had "To Be Filed" scribbled on its side. "Hmm, I know it's in . . . got it," he said, pulling out a single piece of paper. "Read this, starting from here," he said, handing me the paper.

Now what? I thought. Ron got up from his seat and stooped over my shoulder as I read about a mathematical finding discovered over a century ago. The numerological study on the Bible text illustrated incredible patterns in prime numbers. It compiled the sum of the numerical values in words, sentences, paragraphs, passages, and whole books in the original ancient Aramaic and ancient Hebrew texts. According to the article, words, proper names, letters, words that appear more than once, words that appear only once, nouns, and words that weren't nouns all divided by seven. The article then went on to cite numerous examples from both the Old and the New Testaments, pointing out that it would have taken Matthew several months, working eight hours a day, to construct the genealogies in such a numeric pattern, but the names were chosen long before Matthew was born.

In essence, the author of the article proposed that the Bible, in its original language, was a product of a superhuman mathematical mastermind. The article claimed that the Nobel Research Foundation was supplied with more than 43,000 sheets of studies and a challenge to offer a natural explanation or to refute the facts. No one was able to do so.

The chances of these patterns happening by accident were calculated to be 1 in 33 trillion.

By the time I had finished reading the article, all I could hope was that someone had made this up. Just the thought that it was even partially accurate was devastating to me.

Mike must have noted my blank stare. "Do you like science?" he asked.

"Huh?"

"Science. Here's a radical passage that was written more than 2,500 years ago. Try to remember that it was only a few hundred years ago that modern science believed the world was flat, probably supported on the back of a giant turtle or elephant. And who could argue? The world always looks flat to the human eye. But whose eye do you suppose saw this?"

He slid his Bible in front of me and pointed to verses in the book of Isaiah: "Have you not understood from the foundations of the earth? It is He who sits above the *circle* of the earth" (40:21–22).

"And read this—here in what is probably the oldest book in the Bible," Mike said, turning to the book of Job. "He stretches out the north over empty space, and hangs the earth on nothing" (Job 26:7).

"I guess God didn't believe in the turtle theory," Mike said with a smile.

Neither Ron nor I was smiling.

"Are you guys familiar with any of the hundreds of Bible prophecies? Do you know that more than 70 percent of them have already been fulfilled?" Mike went on to cite examples. Some left so little room for interpretation that I had no choice but to agree that the words spoken had indeed been prophetic. How could this have happened? I needed an answer other than the one Mike was proposing.

By the time he finished, my head was spinning. I was both

depressed and awestruck. I wished I had never come to his store for the cool air.

Ron and I talked very little after we left Mike's store, and with the weekend upon us we called it a day. I later found out that after I left, Ron went behind the barn and fell to his knees praying and weeping and changing. He would later tell me that "rose-tinted glasses" had been taken off his eyes and that he saw life clearly for the first time. Answers to unasked questions of social, religious, economic, and political standards and systems filled his young mind. The experience has affected him to this day. He's now a husband, father, and chiropractor living in New England where he's loving his family, his neighbor, and his God.

I have no remembrance of the weekend days flowing into nights. This was true for most of my weekends, but this time it wasn't because of partying with friends. In fact, I did zero socializing. I spent a lot of time reading a Bible that Mike had given me when I left the store. I couldn't put it down. Although my heels were still dug in far enough that I simply couldn't admit that God was the book's Author, I had come to the conclusion that man's signature didn't belong there either. Besides all of the evidence Mike had thrown at us, something else loomed larger and larger as I read on. Too much of man's nature was missing. God was behind everything that went right, and man was responsible for everything that went wrong, just the opposite of the mankind I was familiar with. Man's nature is to lift himself up and put God down. Man *couldn't* have put this together.

Most of my thoughts at that point could be summed up in, *Oh, no . . . it's true.* I could hear a voice inside warning me not to decide against God just because He didn't fit into my plans. I also kept hearing Mike's voice reminding me that not making a decision was equivalent to making one.

I came to the conclusion that I really didn't have a choice I could live with. I couldn't pretend this never happened. But bringing God into my life the way the Bible described would destroy every relationship I had. My friends would want nothing to do with God, and my girlfriend would think I had lost my mind. But could I be happy living a lie?

For the first time in what had to be a decade and a half, I prayed. A simple prayer. I'll never forget it. I figured if God knew what I was thinking and could see through me like glass, I might as well be straight with Him.

Before the words formed in my mouth I had a rush of fear. I was about to lose control of my life, and I didn't want to let go. I'd raced cars at speeds they had no business going, cliff dived into waterfalls, jumped off thousand-foot cliffs with old-style hang gliders, and in ninth grade I'd asked the most beautiful girl in the school to go out on a date, but nothing I had ever done was as scary as this. I was about to throw myself off a building, let go of the trapeze without a net, let go of the steering wheel of my life. I was shaking.

"God," I said, "I don't want You. But apparently I need You. Please give me the desire to want You. I don't really know what You require of me, and even if I did, I probably couldn't do it, so I'll need Your help. Well, I guess that You're the boss now instead of me. Take me . . . I'm Yours.

I told no one of the decision I had made. If I could keep it a secret I would, but I knew my decision would change my life so drastically that my secret would last only as long as I could stay away from people. I spent the night alone in my room, reading a paperback Bible until I fell asleep.

The next morning when I woke up, to my shock, there wasn't anything in the world I wanted more than God. I was hungry to know Him. The desire amazed me. I was still afraid of what my friends would think, but there was something else going on that I couldn't explain. I knew I had a physical body because I could see it and feel it. I knew I had a mind because I was thinking. But I was aware of something else. I didn't know what it was, but it was there. Definitely there. I thought about things nobody had ever spoken to me about. I went from thinking about God none of the time to thinking about Him constantly.

And the following day, Monday, I found myself knocking on Mike's door. He answered and welcomed me in.

At forty-four, Mike was exactly twice my age. He dressed well; I was wearing the same tank top and torn shorts I'd had on the day before. Mike knew the Bible inside and out; I had been reading it for less than a day. Mike's career had been buying and selling stocks and other intangible, invisible goods; I worked with my hands. He had almost no knowledge of sports and had never engaged in any athletics; I was a jock. He preferred the indoors; I needed to be outside, mountain climbing, hunting, and cliff diving with friends. He was automatic; I was stick shift. But at that moment I felt a connection. He might be an eye and I a callus, but we were now members of the same body.

When I told Mike that I had turned to God, he smiled and nodded approvingly as if something he had already known was confirmed.

"Now what do I do?" I said.

The man who hadn't been able to shut up for the last two weeks suddenly delivered an economy of three words that jolted through me.

"Diligently seek God," Mike said.

He had no idea what the weight of those three words meant to me, but I knew instantly.

Two years earlier, on a visit home from college, I had broken the chain on my motorcycle. Without the monetary means to replace the chain and get back upstate to school, and with a sudden determination not to except the monies offered by my parents or grandparents,

I decided to take a week off and earn the money for myself. I loved my family but felt the need to be responsible for myself this time.

The next day, turning down one good friend's offer to hang out and party and another friend's tempting invitation to "get it on" with her, I walked more than ten miles with nothing more than a canteen of water and a strange voice in my ear that continued to tell me to *diligently seek work*. I first went to the corner gas station, hoping I could pump gas. The response was, "Not right now, but fill out this application and when we have an opening, we'll call." Undeterred and encouraged by that small voice, I continued.

Diligently seek work.

I stopped at every retail store, delicatessen, grocery store, lumberyard, and marina, all the time thinking that *I* was telling myself to *diligently seek work*. I pressed on until I finally convinced a shipyard foreman to allow me to scrape barnacles off boat bottoms.

The instant Mike said, "Diligently seek God," the memory and meaning of that day were illuminated before me like a drive-in theater screen. In that very second, I knew without a doubt that there was a God and that He had been involved in my life long before I ever met Mike and heard his apologetics.

When I saw Ron, I told him of my weekend and of the brief conversation I had just had with Mike. He told me that he had also made a decision to go with God. This comforted me and made me wonder if maybe more of my friends would understand and have similar experiences.

• • •

July 10, 1977, a Sunday morning. Sunday meant nothing to me, just another day in the week. The commitment I'd made was to God, not to man, and I was in no hurry to shackle myself with a whole new set of rules and regulations just because of tradition. As far as learning more about the Bible and the Christian life went, earlier in the week Mike had generously agreed to meet with me every Monday night to study the Bible one on one or with whoever might show up. I felt safe with Mike. He'd told me that fellowship with other Christians would come in time and that God would speak to me as to when and where. In the meantime I would pray and read the Bible.

That Sunday, I worked at the barn all day. With the exception of the deli clerk at lunchtime and dinner, I didn't see anyone all day, not even Ron, who had taken the day off. At ten that night I was busy carpeting the stairway when I heard the familiar sound of my best friend's Kawasaki Z-1000 come up the driveway.

I had known Rich Ortner since ninth grade when we were on the cross-country team together. We had been best friends ever since. When we were twenty, we moved to Colorado after seeing *Jeremiah Johnson*, a movie about a man who'd had enough of civilization and went to live in the Rocky Mountains. We looked at each other and said, "Let's go," and we did just that. We found a little log shed with a wood stove and stayed there most of the fall and into the winter. We spent our days hunting, hiking, playing chess, reading old copies of *Reader's Digest*, chopping wood, and drinking hot chocolate. We bathed in nearby hot springs that bubbled out of the ground at 130 degrees and feasted every day on mule deer. We were already best friends, but those two seasons together in the mountains forged an unbreakable bond between us.

That Sunday night in July he had just driven down from his parents' upstate home. Earlier that day, Rich had begun clearing land on some of his father's acreage for a log cabin he planned on building.

He wanted to tell me about it right away, so he detoured to Glen Cove, where he knew I would still be working.

"What do you have to do, open tomorrow?" Rich said, standing in the doorway.

"Hey, Rich. I just wanted to finish these stairs and then—"

"Lose those tools, ya maniac. Let's get a beer."

I stared at him for all of five seconds, dropped my tool belt on the stairs, shut off the light, and locked the door. We walked to a nearby bar, where we ordered a couple of beers and played a game of eight-ball pool. Rich won. We got a refill on the beers and found a seat at a table by a window.

"You know that guy, Mike, I told you about? The Jesus guy?" I said, knowing I needed to talk about my decision with my best friend, but not knowing where to start.

"Yeah. Now what's he tellin' you, that you're possessed but you don't have to worry 'cause he's an exorcist?"

I laughed and went on to tell him all I could remember of that day Ron and I first had lunch in the bookstore. After I could no longer stand keeping it in, I told him that I now believed in God.

"You?" he said, as astonished as I had ever seen him.

"Yeah, why not?"

"I just can't believe you, of all people . . . wait a minute, is this guy a Jehovah's Witness? They're always coming around the house and—"

"No," I said.

Rich shook his head and sat back in his seat. Then he said something I'll never forget: "I don't think I'm ready for this."

"It's not a matter of getting ready. You don't get ready for God. You give yourself to God, and He gets you ready for whatever."

"Well, then, I don't think I'm ready to be gotten ready."

"That's a decision only you can make," I said, suddenly realizing that I was doing to Rich what Mike had done to me. "You might have another fifty years to decide, but you might also be dead an hour from now. There are no guarantees."

He stared at me for a long moment before he finally shrugged his shoulders and said, "Yeah, that's true. Let's have another game of pool."

We played a last game of pool and then walked back to the barn. Rich put his arm around my shoulder as we walked the last few feet to my car. "Which way?" he asked. "The highway or the back road?"

"Whatever," I said.

"I'll follow you," he said, then straddled his bike.

It was a beautiful night and I wished I still had my Honda 750. I had recently sold it, thinking I had already had more lives than a cat on it, and going down hard with it was only a question of when. As I drove out of the driveway and onto the street, the single lamp of Rich's bike followed closely. I made a right and then a left, deciding to take the back road home.

At a red light, the car bumped forward. I looked in the rearview mirror and saw Rich bumping me with his front tire and yelling at me to go through the light. It was about one in the morning, and there wasn't any traffic moving in any direction as far as we could see. The light turned green and I went.

I was driving a Volkswagen station wagon called a square back. It didn't have much speed or power, and by the time I reached a steep hill about a quarter mile from the light, Rich decided to pass me. He probably figured the hill would slow me down even more and it was time for me to follow him.

I heard the Kawasaki downshift and then throttle up. Rich and I had ridden with each other for the past four years, and during that time we had done some pretty crazy things, sometimes on wet or sandy roads. The hill was neither wet nor sandy. Dry and relatively smooth. Rich was simply passing me on the left and with enough gas to emphasize the mismatch of the two vehicles.

The next moment has played in my mind countless times during the last twenty years and always in slow motion. I heard the roar of the powerful bike as Rich gunned the throttle. I looked out my side window to watch the bike pass me by, but it never did. Somehow, Rich had traveled wide and his front tire scraped the curb, causing the tire to jump. He stood up slightly, trying to compensate and keep balance. Then the back tire scraped, jumping up as the front tire had and bumping Rich off the bike, though he still held the handlebars. The bike went down on its left side, skidding and sparking along the curb but still in the street. Rich, however, was not in the street. He was sliding on top of the curb until he was suddenly stopped by a telephone pole. The bike continued up the hill for another couple of hundred feet.

I screamed Rich's name as I slammed on the brake. When the car slowed down enough, I jumped out, letting it find its own way to stop up on the sidewalk. I ran to him, but for all the good it did I might just as well have walked. His helmet had broken off, and his glasses were gone. He looked upward with a blank stare. I screamed at him again and again, believing he was unconscious. I knew that any second he was going to blink. I grabbed his shoulders and pulled him toward me. His head hung back limp.

Hyperventilating hysterically, I ran toward a car that had just come out of a side street near where the bike rested. I ran in front of the car, forcing it to either stop or hit me, then pounded my two fists onto the front hood.

"There's been an accident," I screamed as loudly as I could to the two terrified people behind the windshield. I pointed to the bike in the street. "I need a telephone," I cried. The driver pointed to a pay phone directly across the street. I hadn't even noticed it. I ran to it and dialed 911.

By the time I was halfway back to Rich, I could already hear the sirens and see the lights coming from the city below. Two minutes later the site was sprawling with police cars and paramedics. After failing to find a pulse, one of the paramedics held a small mirror by Rich's nose. He looked at me and then at an officer. As they looked at each other, I heard the unspoken words, but refused to accept them. They knew he was gone and wasn't coming back, regardless of any extreme efforts on their part. Nonetheless, they raced Rich into the ambulance and sped him off to the hospital.

I followed behind the ambulance, screaming at God. "What have You done? What are You doing? Why Rich? Why?" I yelled again and again. The fact that an hour ago I had told Rich that he might have only another hour to live hadn't escaped me. At first I didn't even consider that God might have used me to reach out to Rich, knowing his time on this planet had come to an end. Instead, I wondered if I should dare ever talk to *anyone* about God again. Had I become some kind of last-chance prophet? A messenger boy for the Grim Reaper?

At the Glen Cove Hospital emergency room, Rich was rushed through a set of double swinging doors. I was not allowed to follow. A nurse intercepted me and tried to console me. Soon, a doctor appeared through the doors and confirmed Rich's death. He then asked if I would inform my friend's parents of the accident. I agreed, but in the phone conversation all I could tell Rich's father was that Rich had been in a bike accident and that he needed to come as soon as possible. I found that I wasn't very good at delivering bad news, especially telling a family so near and dear to me that their only son had just died.

Though I didn't understand why Rich had to die, I held onto my newfound belief in God, and my faith grew. It wasn't until after Robyn's death that God revealed to me why these tragedies must happen.

CHAPTER 18

WHY TRUST GOD AFTER THIS?

(CINDY)

Just a couple of months before Bill had his encounter with God in 1977, I, too, had an experience that brought me to the faith I have today. And just like Bill, I was not on any quest for God or searching for my purpose in the universe. God made the first move. And had He not, I would never have written a letter to Verma Harrison in the first place.

My mother faithfully took my brothers and me to church every Sunday. Well, almost every Sunday. She wasn't what I would call very religious, but apparently she thought going to church it was important because I remember going often.

When I was twelve, my father's mother took my brother Ray and me to her birthplace in the former Yugoslavia, with a stop in Rome, Italy. There we saw the Vatican and St. Peter's. I felt so little in that huge cathedral. I also felt pretty insignificant as I viewed the pope and the swarm of religious folk all about me who had also made the pilgrimage. Somehow, this trip made God seem very far away from me since I was not a religious person and had no desire to be.

If anyone had asked me whether I believed in God, I would have said, "Yes." God, however, was not a central character in the story of my life or at least not one that I was aware of. Perhaps that's because going to church and participating in religious instruction classes did more to increase my knowledge of religion, but not of God. I supposed He was there, somewhere, overseeing things and keeping tabs on how many prayers the older women were reciting. I figured He was in heaven, wherever and whatever that was, and I would meet Him when I died. But I didn't spend much time, if any, thinking about Him.

Not that I was cynical. I just didn't know God could be part of my everyday life. I guess I approached the matter of God the way I approached my school subjects: I did what I thought I *had* to do, but would have much rather been doing what I *wanted* to do. Religion was just another subject sitting on the bookshelf of my mind, like math or history. I opened those books only when I had to.

When I was about fourteen, I stopped going to church altogether. On Easter, 1977, when I was sixteen and a sophomore in high school, I watched the television movie *Jesus of Nazareth* with my family. Then I realized that I knew almost nothing about what Jesus had done or taught.

Sitting in my usual spot in front of the piano bench on the floor in our living room, I listened to the words of the actor who was supposed to be Jesus Christ. As I listened to him talking about "loving your brother from your heart" and "looking after others' needs before your own," I became aware of how little my own life lined up with Jesus' teachings about relationships. In my self-conscious teenage world, I was the number one person in my life—and that seemed to be the norm for those around me too. Suddenly what I was hearing sounded so right, so simple. What if people did just what this man said? Wouldn't they all be able to get along if they did? And what about the words he spoke about God as a loving Father, always near, always caring? Could it be true that *God* cared for *me?*

As the movie approached its conclusion, I went up to my bedroom. Actually I ran up, crying. I was very upset that this gentle, loving, and wise teacher was being crucified, and I couldn't bear to watch any more of the movie. But what I *had* seen and heard spoke volumes to my heart about a deep and beautiful love and about a very human and very reachable Jesus.

I began thinking about my religious upbringing, with its rules and intimidating confessionals, its somber and mysterious rituals. Then my visit to St. Peter's in Rome flashed through my mind. How far away God had seemed to me then. I sat on the floor in the dark, thinking, trying to figure out my thoughts and feelings, and although I didn't recognize it as such at the time, the beginnings of faith were stirring inside me. I found myself saying aloud, "You are real," and marveled at the thought. I had never simply spoken to God from my own heart, from my own formulated thoughts.

As children, we were taught the prayers we were supposed to say: "Our Father who art in heaven, hallowed be Thy name . . ." (When I was young, I wondered what in the world "hallowed" meant.) I think now that Jesus meant for those words to be a model of how to focus when we pray. I believe that He delights when we deviate from form in order to better express what's really in our hearts. We are unique individuals, and the expression of our thoughts in prayer will also be individually unique. I don't think He meant for us to offer Him lip service by mindlessly reciting the words by rote. (Wouldn't it be weird if my husband came home from work and all my kids and I recited only selected words to him, all in unison, and rarely deviated from day to day as the only form of communication with him?)

Anyway, speaking to God in conversational form was something new and alive to me. And when I said those words, a Presence filled my room. That's the only way I can describe it. I didn't see anything. I didn't hear anything. I didn't feel any physical sensations. But I felt like a piece of glass, totally transparent, completely known. This Presence saw and understood all of my lifelong thoughts, understood all of my hurts and the many times I had felt misunderstood. Unseen eyes penetrated who I was and poured out compassion on me. Though I was utterly exposed, I felt totally secure, flooded with calm, with tranquillity. I began to cry in awe.

At that moment it was as if someone removed a very heavy backpack from my shoulders. And I knew what that backpack was. It was all the wrongs I had done in my life. Every selfish act. It was a weight I hadn't known I was carrying, but apparently God didn't want me carrying it any longer.

Suddenly I felt free. And it seemed so right, as though the deepest part of me was home. I was more alive than ever before. In fact, I was convinced that, before, I had only existed, but now I had life. Plugged into a reality I had never known. Connected. I said something like, "I didn't know," or "I never knew You." Then a message came to my mind. Not audibly, but as clear as if it had been spoken aloud. *Come.* Then I was on my knees, reaching up into the dark. "I don't know where I'm going," I said, "but I want to be where You are."

. . .

For days afterward, all these emotions and thoughts lingered. I had a purpose. I wanted to stay close to this Presence who knew me and loved me. I would give Him my life and follow wherever He would lead.

I became hungry to hear His words and know His thoughts, so I began to read my mother's Bible. It was a huge book with pictures that looked as if they came from the Renaissance period. It had always looked so intimidating, and I didn't understand much at first. But I'd come home from school, sit on my bed, and read from the New Testament.

As I read, it seemed as though Jesus Himself was standing before me, speaking those words into my mind and deep into my heart. I knew God was with me, and I was confident that He was there to stay, just a whisper away.

To anyone observing me, my life might not have seemed to change much. But so much had changed inside me. One major change was that I was less concerned about pleasing myself and doing things my way and more concerned about looking out for others' interests. I became aware of the kids who were looked down upon by others for not being "cool"; I began to care about *their* feelings and tried to befriend some who regularly walked to class alone. I wondered if preoccupation with myself was part of the weight in the "backpack" that had been lifted from me. Now I looked upon others with new eyes. I had a brand-new love and respect for them. I recognized that the Love that loved me also loved them. And I wanted to show this love to others through my actions.

I had no understanding of how faith worked, however, and I had much to learn about the relationship between God and mankind. When I met Bill three years later, he invited me to his church in Glen Cove. There, I was like a dry sponge soaking up water. I was so hungry for knowledge about God and His ways that when the pastor taught from the Bible, I drank deeply.

•   •   •

This first encounter with God came at a time in my life when boys and dating were somewhere at the top of the list of priorities for my friends and me. But having just been filled with God's love, I put to rest my personal pursuit for "Mr. Right." My soul had met its truest love, and I was convinced that no man could love me like that.

In December 1981, six days before my nineteenth birthday, I met Bill. It was a Saturday, and I had decided to visit a coffeehouse in Glen Cove that evening. I had seen a flyer in a bookstore advertising that a Christian musician I had seen and enjoyed before would be playing there. A friend said he'd meet me there, but sometime in the afternoon he called to say he wasn't feeling well and wasn't going to make it. He was also expecting to see another one of his friends at the coffeehouse that night and had tried unsuccessfully to reach him by phone to tell him he was sick. He asked if I would look for his friend and give him that message. He described his friend for me: "He's at least six feet tall, has brown hair and a beard, and his name is Bill Griffiths."

I found Bill during intermission. He was in his midtwenties and had wonderful, warm, intelligent-looking brown eyes. At the end of the evening we chatted a bit, and he asked for my phone number.

Over the next few weeks, we became friends. Bill was very athletic, funny, and the outdoors type. Best of all, he also had a passion for God. He led a weekly Bible study at his church and invited me to attend. He was (and still is) a great storyteller. And he could make the Bible come alive. We talked a lot about God and eventually played our guitars and sang together of Him.

We saw a filmstrip called *The Champion* that portrayed, in cartoon form, the final week of the life of Christ. The piece had a musical accompaniment of six songs. We learned the songs on our guitars and began to visit places such as the Human Resource Center for disabled children, schools, and churches to show the filmstrip and sing the songs live. We had a common desire to help others know this God who had invaded our lives with His goodness.

A little more than a year after we met, Bill and I were married. That was nineteen years ago. I thought I would go into education for the deaf, but we started a family when Stephen was born a year and a half into our marriage. I left thoughts of school and work behind as I gazed into my baby's face. I wanted to be with him, take care of him, and enjoy him while he was little. Motherhood/Domestic Engineer became my "career," and I have not regretted that decision to this day. By the time Stephen was ten, Robyn, Luke, Willy, Peter, and Summer had joined him. My heart was so full. So were the laundry baskets and the sink!

. . .

I'm no Bible scholar or theologian, but I found that keeping my nose in the Bible and growing in my knowledge of the Scriptures helped me stay centered in a life full of responsibilities as wife and mother. I desperately needed to keep the connection with *the* Source of wisdom, joy, rest, and love, and I purposed to spend time alone with God and meditate on the truth of the Scriptures regularly. As I did this and lived out what I learned there, I maintained a relationship with Him that continued to move the deepest part of me and give me great joy.

Loving God was easy; after all, I realized that He loved me first. But trials still came my way, as they do to all of us in a world that is far from perfect. Oftentimes I was bewildered about how God could let something happen the way it was happening; then I would remember His love and trust once again. Sometimes following God's path has been so contrary to my feelings that it has been downright painful, but ultimately the rewards have been worth it.

I often compare this exercise of my will to the exercise of my body. Usually I exercise six mornings a week. On three of those days I run, and on three I do weight-bearing exercises. Rarely do I *feel* like maintaining the discipline of lifting weights or emerging from my warm bed to pull on my running gear and greet a dark, chilly morning. I do it because I have faith that a greater good will come. Through time, perseverance, and patience, I will reap the benefits. Time, perseverance, patience, *and* resistance. It's similar with faith. Just as I use the resistance of weights to increase my physical strength, so I see the (resistance of) trials that come my way as spiritual weights to strengthen my faith. They help me press closer to God and trust Him more as He brings me through another hard time.

Not that I've always trusted Him so easily. Certainly there have been times when I've complained and been frustrated. But the Scriptures tell me to "trust in the LORD with all your heart, and do not lean on your own understanding. In all your ways acknowledge Him, and He will make your paths straight" (Prov. 3:5–6). This passage has helped me because it means that I can rest from trying to figure everything out when there's a distressing situation. I can lift the weight of my trial up to God, by faith, and respond as He would have me respond. Then I will see it work out in the best possible way, which is usually not *my* idea of what's best. But I'm learning that that's okay because God's wisdom is so much greater than ours.

Since God is truth, I figure that when we disagree about how something should be done, I'm the one who needs to get a new perspective. How comforting it is to know that, no matter what the situation, His way is always best. Doing things God's way is not the easiest way, but it has always been the best way for me. Difficulties that seemed like insurmountable boulders in my path have been transformed into stepping-stones to higher ground as I chose to follow Him and depend on *His* strength and wisdom to lead. Eventually He brings me out of the muck and mire of the valley to the mountaintop, where the air is clear and the view magnificent. Where I am surrounded by joy and well-being and peace. But I can't trust and follow Him if I don't know Him. So my prayer has always been, "Let me know You more."

I spent hours in prayer, hours in His presence, and hours in the Bible. I learned what it is like to play and jump and splash in Rivers of Life because that was how I lived, for the most part. And God was still changing me, always leading me upward in my understanding of life and love. As a result, my heart was full of joy and thankfulness, even when I was up to my ears in diapers. Even when I was confined to my house because of sick children and a husband who worked such long hours for us that he had no time or energy left to give me a break with the little ones.

Trials, no matter how severe, can turn to gold. And that's a promise from the One who is stronger than death itself. In the New Testament, Romans 8:28 states, "God causes *all* things to work together for good to those who love God, to those who are called according to His purpose" (emphasis added).

By the time June 28, 1996, rolled around, I had spent years growing closer to the Lover of my soul. Now, more fervently than ever, I would hold fast to His promises, knowing that I would need every ounce of His grace and love to see me through.

PART 4

FINDING OUR WAY

CHAPTER 19

LIFE WITHOUT ROBYN

(CINDY)

After the commotion of that first week, we tried to make things as normal as possible for the children. For the next few weeks, with both my emotional and physical energy levels at a low, I continued to have someone over every weekday morning to help me get the day started. After several weeks, I was on my own again. I was glad it was summer since that meant a much less demanding schedule. At the same time, I needed some kind of routine to busy my mind.

Years ago, I read an article about depression in which the writer, who was a psychiatrist at a mental health clinic, said that one of the things they got patients to do was to maintain an exercise program. In addition to the physical benefits, the daily discipline gave the patient a sense of control over *something* in the midst of a world that was, or seemed, out of control, which was usually a big part of why the person was depressed in the first place. Talk about a loss of control. *That* certainly described me. When I would feel depressed and sluggish, I'd get up and exercise anyway, reminding myself of the article I had read.

Focusing on the necessary family tasks and caring for the children also kept my mind occupied and helped me avoid some depression when the waves of grief washed over me. At times, however, I would simply be overcome with emotion. When that happened, I went to my room and had a good cry.

One evening, I was reading through a book about the grieving process and came to a chapter that mentioned the importance of saying good-bye to the one who was gone. When I read it, I promptly threw the book across the room in disgust and anger. I was so sure in my heart that my relationships with Robyn and my mother were not over, but were merely on hold for a while, that I could not stomach the idea of saying good-bye. "See you later" was more like it. The next day, however, I reread that part, and I understood that the author was encouraging people to come to terms with the fact that their loved one would never be coming back. The good-bye was merely a reality check. Apparently there are those who leave the bedcovers turned down or a favorite book open on the desk just in case the loved one returns. I knew Robyn and my mother were not coming back.

The book also spoke of the inevitable and necessary forming of new habits. Oh, how I wanted to rebel against this idea. Part of me didn't want "new habits." But I had no choice. There was no going around the storm; I had to walk through it one step at a time. And there would be no avoiding the inevitable changes in the landscape once the tidal floods receded. Robyn and Mom were not going to be there tomorrow or the next day or the next. Yes, indeed, things were going to be *very* different, for these dear ones had taken up such a large place in my heart and thoughts.

Things that had been automatic became daggers in my flesh.

Getting ready for dinner—we needed to count seven of everything and not eight anymore. Finding some of her clothes in the laundry room and knowing that she'd never wear them again. Coming upon one of her books or toys. These things happened every day for a long time.

Robyn loved animals. She always had rabbits and/or guinea pigs. One of her guinea pigs was pregnant when she left for Salt Lake City, and in one of our phone calls while she was on the road, she asked me to take pictures of the babies when they arrived and send them to her so she could name them.

When they were born, I was excited for about three seconds till I realized that Robyn and I couldn't rejoice together. The excitement vanished and left me standing, once again, in a vacuum. I coddled those little critters as if they were orphans who would never get to know their mama.

One day I took the children to Toys "R" Us to buy several birthday gifts. As I walked around the store, I saw Robyn everywhere. How could these sweet, fun, and sometimes cuddly objects have the power to torment me? Yet my heart was pierced with the memory of Robyn and her first doll, which she named Cindy-baby; Robyn and her pink training wheeler when she was six; her first roller skates when she was seven. With each remembrance something was sucked out of me again and again, when I thought there couldn't possibly be anything left to be taken. I fought back the tears. Then I reminded myself that God had not abdicated His throne. Oh, to know that Someone was still in control! A few minutes after that, I bumped into a friend in one of the aisles. We talked of the love and faithfulness of God, and I felt better. Our meeting was no accident.

In addition to learning to cope with life without Robyn, I faced the challenge of trying to help the rest of our children understand what was happening, both externally and internally. It was probably hardest on Stephen, the oldest, who had the most memories. He and Robyn were our first two and were close, with a significant camaraderie between them. Turning thirteen in the midst of this tumultuous time, Stephen was visibly the most emotional one at the loss of his sister.

One evening at bedtime we heard him crying. Bill went to his room to talk with him. When he returned to our room, he said that Stephen had calculated that if he lived "x" amount of years, it would be so many years without Robyn and he was afraid he'd forget her. He was distraught that he would have known her only 10 percent of his life, as he put it.

The other children, probably because they were so young, did not demonstrate much emotion. However, I noticed that when they saw me upset, they became sullen. And when I was upbeat, they were more apt to be that way too. Their little hearts mirrored my emotions to some degree, so I tried to be careful not to lose control in their presence. I didn't think I should hide all my pain from them since that might be doing them an injustice in the long run. Better to see the reality that life can sometimes hurt and this is how we walk through it than to be shielded from life's harsh dealings and thus unequipped when they're no longer under the shadow of my wing.

I would talk about Robyn and about the truth of the Scriptures. I also asked them questions about their feelings. I didn't want to find out years later that they were emotionally harmed because of what happened. I still hope that. I knew they needed lots of physical contact, an ever-listening ear, and tons of TLC.

Three-year-old Summer had shared a room with Robyn. Until just a couple of months before the accident, she would fall asleep in her own bed and wake up in Robyn's. At some point in her sleep cycle, she'd wake up and crawl into Robyn's bed, virtually *every* night. Until Bill built a loft for Robyn's bed in their room, the girls slept in the same twin bed. I held Summer often, comforting her with physical closeness.

Walking through the storm with the children was not entirely bad. The good news was that I knew the Bible, and I shared its timeless truths with them again and again. I can never say enough about what the Bible has done to keep me sane, and how I have used its message to counsel my kids. I didn't need to make up any fantasy about Robyn and Grandma becoming our guardian angels. The Scriptures clearly state that angels are angels and people are people. Although it was well intended, it was not comforting to me to hear people say that this was what they'd become. The Bible indicates that because God is the Creator, He is going to continue to create, and His children will have the responsibility and privilege of caring for His creation with Him. We are going to continue to be human, only with a quality of life that our limited existence "down" here on earth can never experience.

I told the children that someday we will be reunited with those who have gone before us, and we will live together in the kind of place that all of us here on earth long for in our hearts, but can't find. We can't find it because it's not here; it's there. I also told them that we on earth think we know how to throw a good party. Well, we "ain't seen nothin' yet." God is going to throw the best party the universe has ever known. And for those who walk with Him now, the hors d'oeuvres are already being served. When opportunity allowed, I tried to communicate these things to the kids, and I listened when they were ready to talk. I prayed for them then—and still do—concerning the effects of Robyn's absence.

. . .

In addition to the Bible, one book in particular helped me through that first summer. I should say it helped me through the evenings, just before I fell asleep, because nighttime was the hardest time. Without the distractions of the day, thoughts of Robyn circled through the dark, quiet hours. When I got into bed each night, for ten or fifteen minutes I would read from *Heaven, Your Real Home* by Joni Eareckson Tada. Sometimes it would actually get me excited about where Robyn and my mom were. (How wonderful to be able to feel *joy* in the midst of the fire.) And I would usually fall into a restful sleep afterward.

Several times I dreamed of Robyn, and when I woke up, I was devastated. I had just seen her, and she seemed so alive, so close. All I could think of was holding her again.

One night, in late July, I was sitting on my bed in the dark, just before turning in for the night. I was contemplating the idea that God had taken me up on my offer of "even the children" for His glory. As I sat there considering my prayers of years gone by—that none of my life would be for me, but all of it for Him—an indignant feeling welled up inside me. Anger pressed upon me like water bearing down upon a door that I was desperately trying to keep closed. *How dare You!* I thought. *With all I've done for You. With all I've given You already. I have withheld nothing from You, and yet You ripped my heart out!* Part of me wanted to open up this door, if only to relieve the pressure. Another part of me thought, *No, my God is good. "Though He slay me, yet will I trust in Him." I will not rise up against Him.*

Consumed with this inner struggling, I whispered into the dark, "I can't believe You really did this. I can't believe You really allowed this to happen. I don't want to be embittered against You. I know there is no greater love than Yours. It's just that *You* had the power to prevent this." Stunned, I stated, "I can't believe You actually took me up on my offer."

Even as I said these things, I received a response. Words were carried to my mind on a wave of compassion and understanding: *Would you have preferred that I asked?*

Upon hearing this, I immediately thought of Abraham in the book of Genesis. Abraham waited a long time for a son. In fact, he was quite old when he finally looked upon little Isaac, the child who had been promised to him by God many years before. Then while Isaac was still a boy, God spoke to Abraham and told him to take his son to Mount Horeb and sacrifice him. God had never asked for a human sacrifice; nevertheless, Abraham knew it was the God he loved who had spoken to him. He did not understand how God could ask such a thing of him. After all, God had told him that through Isaac, he, Abraham, would be the father of many nations. How could that possibly be if God required him to destroy the one through whom His promise was to be fulfilled?

As it turned out, the whole ordeal was a test for Abraham. When he arrived at the appointed place and prepared his son as he would an animal sacrifice, binding him on a stone altar, he heard the voice of God telling him not to harm the boy. And then Abraham heard the sound of a ram rustling in the bushes. It had been caught by its horns, and Abraham knew that it was God's provision for the sacrifice. God had not intended Abraham to take the life of his son. But He was searching out Abraham's heart to see if he would trust and obey Him, no matter what.

What kind of loving God would do something so cruel, some may ask, especially to such a faithful servant? But I have come to know, both through the Scriptures and through personal experience, that God is interested in a relationship with us. And how can we have such a relationship, how can we love Him, if there is no choice *not to?* Love is a choice. Love is sacrifice. And love is best proved in the most trying circumstances. The light shines best in the darkness, and Abraham's love for God was proved in the most difficult decision of his life.

That period of time during which he knew he was going to give his son had to have been a time of excruciating mental torment for Abraham.

It was not a matter of minutes between his decision and the action. He had to prepare everything and then travel with Isaac to Mount Horeb. Then they climbed the mountain together, where Abraham prepared the altar of sacrifice. There was plenty of time to change his mind—and plenty of time to agonize over what he was about to do.

That night, the thought of Abraham's agony actually brought me instant relief. If God had asked me to make a choice, like Abraham had to make, I don't know how I could have responded willingly. Would I have been able to live up to my own confession of loyalty, zealously uttered in moments of deep spiritual intimacy with the One I claim to love above anything else in life? If God had a purpose in allowing all this to happen, as I believed He did, then ideally I would give Him anything He required of me.

Yet would I? In comparing my situation to Abraham's, I saw the mercy of God that He did not ask me first and leave such a decision up to me. And in recognizing that mercy, my heart was broken, and I tearfully lifted up my voice in thanks and praise to Him. I had cried out to God for help, and He had spoken into the darkness of my soul and brought peace. Then I prayed, as I had before, that He would use for good all the darkness into which we had been flung, knowing again that He could bring life from death and light from darkness.

With gratitude and humility, I fell asleep.

• • •

One day as I was cutting away some spent flowers in the backyard, I thought about Jesus' words in John 15:1–4 (NIV):

I am the true vine and my Father is the gardener. He cuts off every branch in me that bears no fruit, while every branch that does bear fruit he trims clean so that it will be even more fruitful. You are already clean because of the word I have spoken to you. Remain in me, and I will remain in you. No branch can bear fruit by itself; it must remain in the vine. Neither can you bear fruit unless you remain in me.

God is the Gardener, and we are the plants. He will prune us at times to cause more fruit to grow in our lives.

As I thought about this, I considered my garden. Sometimes I cut away branches and stems that are dead and therefore useless. But sometimes I cut away living parts of a plant in order to get the plant to grow differently, in order to produce more abundance. What if a plant could tell me just how that process feels? Amputation is what it is. Yet if I know what I'm doing, it will be for the good of the plant.

Similar to a natural gardener, God tends us and does His part to see that we produce abundance with our lives. But to help us do that, He sometimes needs to prune us. Not only does He remove what is worthless, but also at times He takes away what is a living part of us—something that may be important to us. Again, that's amputation, and it hurts.

The key for me has always been "to abide" in Him or, as the verses from John 15 say, "to remain" in Him. Without Him, very little makes sense to me. I know my best interests as well as the best interests of others are His concern. When things happen that I don't like or understand, I eventually come to a place of trusting Him to bring about what is best. I can't always see the fruit He's trying to lovingly produce in my life, but I can trust Him that it will happen as I yield to the pruning process. I may not know what the future holds, but I know who holds the future.

This understanding brought me tremendous peace of mind during that summer, and until this very day, concerning the living, thriving parts of me that were removed from my life on June 28, 1996.

And parts of me they were, my mother and my daughter. Sometimes I didn't know where my heart ended and theirs began. Our lives and our love were so interwoven that losing them was amputation.

I tried to keep my thoughts centered upon the timeless truths of the Bible. I sang songs of God's love and faithfulness. I pumped this kind of music through my house and in the car while driving. And when the grief would come and knock me to the ground, I was aware that I did not cry alone. To know that my sorrow touches the heart of God is an awesome thing to me. The psalmist said of the Lord, "You keep track of all my sorrows. You have collected all my tears in your bottle. You have recorded each one in your book" (Ps. 56:8 NLT). That knowledge makes me feel loved in a way I cannot describe.

When I was a child, we had one of those blow-up punching bags with sand in the bottom so that it always returned to an upright position. Ours was a clown, and I can remember slamming that thing as hard as I could. It would go down, but inevitably it would rise again. That's what I have experienced with grief. Grief came (and still does) and hit us hard. We were knocked down, but we didn't remain there. We kept popping back up. Just as the sand in the bottom of the punching bag constantly righted it, so the truth of the Word of God kept us grounded and stabilized so that we could not remain defeated by death's vicious blows. Again, I think of Scripture: "We do not grieve as those who have no hope" (1 Thess. 4:13, author's paraphrase), and "O Death, where is your sting?" (1 Cor. 15:55 NKJV).

. . .

In mid-August of that first summer, we drove up to New Hampshire for our annual summer vacation with Bill's parents at their lake house.

We all felt the loss of the missing family member and seemed to desire to tenderly love one another through those two weeks.

While there, I penned a letter to the people who had supported us when the nightmare began. One evening at dusk I stationed myself on the cottage porch, which overlooks the southern end of beautiful Lake Sunapee. Now and again, I'd lift moist eyes to gaze upon the tranquil surface of the lake as I wrote:

August 17, 1996

This note comes to you, with much gratitude, for your loving concern and thoughtfulness toward us during this most difficult time. Your love has touched us through your visits, your cards, your beautiful flowers and baskets, your meals, your financial gifts, and the many other ways you showed you cared. All this reaching out has been like salve on the wound, and we are blessed. Thank you.

We will always remember June 28, 1996, as a horrible, yet glorious day. Horrible because of the tragedy. Horrible because of the wound inflicted upon us as death stole our loving mother (in-law) and our precious, precious daughter, Robyn, and left our hearts bleeding and in shreds. Horrible when we think of all we've lost!

How can it be that we no longer see Robyn flipping on the trampoline or playing with her little sister? Where are the sweet, soft songs our piano sang as her gentle hands danced nimbly across its keys? How can it be that she and I (Cindy) will no longer dance for joy to our favorite songs in my kitchen, as we have countless times before? How she enjoyed her ballet class. How we sang together. How we laughed together. How we enjoyed, together. Together. And now, no longer together.

We see her empty bed at night and ask, "How can all this be real?" We long to hold her again. We long to see the peace in her eyes and the love in her smile. But she's not here. And the pain is beyond anything we've ever known.

Yet, somehow, her absence here serves to solidify our assurance of her presence in another place. We know Robyn and her grandma live, because we know the One who said, "I am the resurrection and the life; he who believes in Me will live, even though he dies" (John 11:25). Robyn and Janice believed in Him. They also experienced the benefits of a relationship with Him while they were here. That means abundant life. That means experiencing some of the peace and joy and beauty of heaven while on earth. It means friendship with the Father. It also means eternal life. They have left the land of the dead (everything here dies) to enter the land of the living, where "He shall wipe away every tear from their eyes; and there shall no longer be any death; there shall no longer be any mourning, or crying, or pain; the first things have passed away" (Revelation 21:4).

Just as an acorn is changed into the mighty oak, or the caterpillar into a butterfly, Robyn and her grandma have been changed. They are still themselves, only better, with new bodies that cannot grow old and die. This is why I used the word *glorious* before. It says in the Bible, "No eye has seen, no ear has heard, no mind has conceived what God has prepared for those who love Him" (1 Corinthians 2:9 NIV).

You know, if it weren't for Jacques Cousteau and other oceanographers, few of us would know about life in the silent depths of the sea. Yet in the dark, and in the deep, there is movement. There's a whole world teeming with life. And just as the sea is full of hidden secrets, this life of ours is rich with secrets too. Hidden plans wrought in perfect love and faithfulness by an all-loving and wise God. A God who seems so silent, unless we allow ourselves to listen. A God who loves so deeply that He gave His own Son to pay

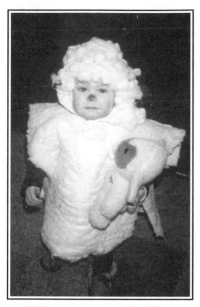

Robyn at 16 months old—
"Our Little Lamb."

Robyn, 6 years old, with Bill's parents,
Bill and Dorothy, and brothers Willy
and Stephen.

Piano recital—7 years old in June '92. Sometimes
I made us matching outfits.

My mother and my daughter—so much
love for each other . . . and for me.

Bill and Robyn (8 years
old) getting ready to
square dance with the
Girl Scouts. Robyn
adored her dad. Our dog
Cedar also died in '96.

At 8 years old, Robyn represented hope in a
musical about faith. She seemed to always
have a song in her heart.

Winter of '94—9
years old. Robyn
loved to skate.

The baby-lover.
"The fruit of the spirit is love, joy,
peace . . . gentleness" (Galatians 5:22).

Loving her little sister, Summer,
came naturally for Robyn.

My ladies and me—Robyn's 10th birthday "Princess Party."
I wonder . . . what type of crowns did the Lord reward
them with in heaven? (December '94)

My parents, Joe and Janice Nicolich, on
a Caribbean vacation in 1994—they
had been married for 40 years.

Spring of '94—Robyn (9),
Summer (1), and me. I enjoyed
sewing for the girls.

Stephen (12), Robyn (11), Luke (9), Will (7), and Peter (5)
at Bill's parents' in New Hampshire (February '96).

Ta-da . . . January '96,
11 years old.

Mom and me clowning around. Mom
had a reputation for her joy and
laughter (April '96).

Robyn and Thumper. Robyn's menagerie consisted mainly of rabbits and guinea pigs. She was heartbroken when any of them died. In her room I found letters she wrote to God asking for her deceased pets to be in heaven so she could play with them when she got there.

Her last home-school field trip—to a colonial house in Port Washington. The kids made breads and pies and baked them on an open hearth. Friend Grace is with her. (May '96—11 years old)

Lookin' pretty on our way to her only ballet recital—twenty days before the crash. I refuse to wash her leotard (June '96).

Robyn liked this comfortable, too big dress.
We buried her in it less than a month later (June '96).

Grandmother	Granddaughter
Janice Ann Nicolich	Robyn Snow Griffiths
August 9, 1935–June 28, 1996	December 12, 1984–June 28, 1996

Verma Jean Harvey and me, holding each other as God holds us both. (Wyoming, April '98)

Verma and me singing our hearts out to the Great Comforter and Healer of our souls during a worship service. (April '98)

Me on the shoulder of I-80 in Sidney, Nebraska, the site of the crash (April '98).

a price we could not pay ourselves. A God who wants so desperately for us to return home to Him, where all is safe.

We do not understand all of the *whys* of what has happened, but we know we can, and do, trust the One who holds the keys to life and death. None of us knows what the future holds here, but we can know the One who holds the future. Not merely know about Him—but *know* Him, individually and personally.

This is our hope and our comfort. We know God is sustaining us, and that He will continue to do so. We are grateful, so grateful, for the peace and sanity He gives.

> The steadfast of mind,
> Thou wilt keep in perfect peace,
> Because he trusts in thee.
> Trust in the Lord forever,
> For in God the Lord, we have an
> Everlasting Rock. (Isaiah 26:3–4)

We are so grateful to all of you who have shown us support. We pray God's nearness for each of you. Please continue to pray for us.

Love,
Bill and Cindy
Stephen, Luke, Willy, Peter,
and Summer Griffiths

CHAPTER 20

Strength from Weakness

(Bill)

The fact is, crisis, fear, tragedy, and grief intensified my spiritual senses. I hate to admit it, but as much as I seek peace, contentment, and confidence, these precious conditions tend to relax not only my mind, but also my spirit. I'm definitely a "stronger when weak" person. Throughout the first year after the crash, my prayers were substantially more fervent in both time and intensity than before, and my ears were straining to hear God's voice. My most memorable events were not scheduled on a calendar or delivered in the mail. They came as healing lightbulb revelations that could reach beyond my wounded heart and often numbed mind.

One Sunday our nine-year-old son, Willy, had to stay home from church because of a bad cold, and our seven-year-old, Peter, was envious and upset because he couldn't stay home with him. Willy was going to get to watch cartoons, and to a seven-year-old, that sounded like a lot more fun than church. My challenge was to explain to Peter why going to church was more important than watching the cartoons. Knowing the length of our Sunday morning meetings and Peter's fondness for cartoons, I really didn't think I had a chance, but as his father, I felt the need to bore him with the details.

I began by telling him that sometimes the Bible seems to list items in an order of importance. "For example," I said, "God gave us Ten Commandments. And the third commandment, which is pretty high on the list, tells us to keep the Sabbath day holy. The Sabbath is a day that comes once a week so daddies can rest, gather with others to recognize God for all He's done, and then eat while watching football, baseball, basketball, or in your case . . . cartoons."

At that point Peter cocked his head to the left in the same way our dog Cedar always would when I would try to explain something to him. But all was not lost. Peter had more than twice Cedar's attention span. I just needed to think fast. Then because I realized that Peter was familiar with the Lord's Prayer in Matthew 6, I explained how in that prayer, the first thing we acknowledge is God and the fact that He is our Father; the next thing the prayer teaches us to do is to recognize that God's name is holy and that His kingdom will and should have priority over less important things in our lives, such as our own provisions or "daily bread." We are instructed not to worry about what we are to wear or eat, but to seek first the kingdom of heaven and all these other things will be taken care of. I was losing Peter fast, so I shifted back to the Ten Commandments, reciting the first commandment, then the second, and then the third.

Wham!

I stopped talking and stared blankly ahead as I suddenly realized something I had never heard before. Never. Not in all the Bible studies, conference messages, tapes, and Sunday sermons.

The fact that Peter shrugged his shoulders and shifted his attention elsewhere would have to wait this time. I couldn't break from the hyperfocus I had just slipped into. I had to walk this through.

I quickly realized the first three commandments hold the same information and are in the exact order as the elements of the prayer commonly known as the Lord's Prayer or "Our Father." The material is the same, but the difference in the delivery is stark. As I pressed on, I was flabbergasted to discover that my notion was correct. The entire Ten Commandments were covered in the Lord's Prayer and in nearly the same order.

Then I began to consider how much more desirable it had always been for me to repeat the Lord's Prayer as opposed to the Ten Commandments. I became even more excited as I remembered that the letter of the law kills, but the Spirit gives life. I can find the Ten Commandments downright depressing because without God's grace, I stand condemned by them. The Lord's Prayer, on the other hand, has always refreshed me, clueing me in to the majesty, goodness, and protection of the almighty Father God.

When I finally arrived at the church meeting, I opened my Bible and went through the Ten Commandments and linked them to the Lord's Prayer in my notebook.

The first commandment proclaimed, "I am the LORD thy God . . . thou shalt have no other gods before me." Contrast that with, "Pray then in this way: Our Father, who art in heaven." The first thing I noticed was that there was no "thou shalt not" to turn my face shamefully away from, only a gentle hand that raised my chin to behold the Father.

The second commandment warned me not to take the name of "the LORD thy God in vain." The Lord's Prayer again led me forward by cheering, "Hallowed be Thy name."

The third commandment demanded that I keep holy the Sabbath day, a day of complete rest, so I can meditate on God and seek His will. The penalty for working on the Sabbath, even to light a fire, was death in the Old Testament. In contrast: "Thy kingdom come, Thy will be done."

The fourth commandment told me to obey earthly parents. Just as the Ten Commandments step down from heaven to earthly authority at this point, so does the Lord's Prayer. "On earth as it is in heaven," it says.

The fifth commandment demanded that I do not kill—the ultimate violent act, stemming from severe bitterness, anger, and hate. Again, the New Testament took the positive slant as Jesus told me to ask forgiveness for my trespasses and to forgive those who trespass against me. This, of course, had already helped me forgive Verma Harrison.

The sixth commandment warned me not to commit adultery. "Lead us not into temptation," Jesus said, again going to the root of the problem first.

The seventh commandment, "Thou shalt not steal," was addressed in the Lord's Prayer by praying for my needs, asking Him to provide my "daily bread" and whatever else I need.

The eighth commandment, "Thou shalt not bear false witness against thy neighbour," instructed me not to lie. Jesus prayed, "Deliver us from the evil one," the devil, the very father of lies.

The last two commandments had to do with wanting what isn't mine, commanding me not to covet or want for myself someone else's property or wife. The heart of man is never satisfied; it always wants more and more. This commandment warned me away from wanting other people's property as my own and cautioned me not to build my own kingdom for my own recognition and glory. The Lord's Prayer ends on the same note: "For Thine is the kingdom, the power, and the glory forever."

Wow, that last one gives me goose bumps every time I say it.

That morning, for the first time, I saw the Lord's Prayer as the New Testament's version of the Ten Commandments. The Ten Commandments filtered through grace. Grace makes all the difference.

The lesson I had attempted and failed to give my son Peter wound up refreshing my faith. These insights from God's Word would have been meaningful at any time, but God had shared them with me when I needed to hear them most. At a time when calamity had supercharged my spiritual receptors.

There can be no greater comfort after losing a loved one than to have faith in God's existence strengthened. All that can be seen is but temporary and, in fact, disappearing quickly. All that is eternal is invisible to the physical eye. The next time I am with Robyn, she will be alive and it will be forever.

CHAPTER 21

WHAT ABOUT VERMA HARRISON?

(CINDY)

As the days turned into weeks after death invaded my heart, I began to think more and more about the woman who had driven the van that crashed into my mother, father, and daughter. What was *she* going through now? I knew her name was Verma Harrison. But what kind of person was she? How old were her children? What kind of relationships did she have with them? Did she have a job? Was she an alcoholic? If not, why was she on the road in that condition and so early in the morning? How did she feel about Bill and me? Had she even thought about us? Did she care about what we had lost, or was her heart hardened from a lifestyle of abuse? Obviously she didn't plan for this to happen. What was she thinking now? Right now, this very minute. I wanted to know. I *needed* to know.

Regardless of who she was or what kind of life she had led, she must be walking through her own nightmare. Her life had to have been changed in that instant as well. She would have to live with the knowledge of what she had done, as well as face whatever the justice system had in store for her.

We were told that her van had flipped over twice and lost its roof. She'd received minor injuries, spent a couple of days in the hospital (the same one as my dad), and went to jail, where she also spent a couple of days and was then released. We were told she was in her early thirties and had three children and a live-in boyfriend. She lived in Wyoming and was Native American. The rest was a mystery.

I knew little about her, yet I figured that Verma Harrison must have a lot of problems. Maybe even severe problems, but nothing that love couldn't solve. People often get into bad and addictive habits because somewhere along the line they start believing things about themselves that made them feel worthless. If people believe that they are important, if they feel loved by another and worth *somebody's* time and attention, their own sense of self-worth is nourished. Then when tough times hit, they are less likely to succumb to destructive thoughts, which ultimately breed destructive behaviors. We see all too frequently what happens if that "somebody" does not exist. Children need to be raised on heaping spoonfuls of love, respect, and discipline by the adults in their lives. All kinds of problems arise for the ones who are not.

Did Verma Harrison have a childhood like that? What were the adults like during her growing-up years, and what did they teach her? Maybe they were not really "there" for her. That would not surprise me. Irresponsibility tends to breed irresponsibility, just as love tends to breed love.

Often when I was doing the dishes or driving the car, I'd think of her. It was hard not to. Robyn was always on my mind, and I would replay the mental tapes of what I imagined must have happened on that stretch of Nebraska highway. These scenes would inevitably lead me to the driver. *Who are you, Verma Harrison? Why are you always on my mind?*

And why, oh, why, did God allow this awful thing to happen to us? Surely He hadn't been on vacation. Had He looked away for a few seconds and slipped up on protecting my sweet daughter and mother? No, God is the Almighty, the all-seeing, the omnipotent One. He created all things seen and unseen, the great Choreographer and Composer of life. From the twirling of celestial bodies to the swaying of prairie grasses, from the rumble of thunder on the mountains to the silence of the ocean's depths, from the explosions of atoms in the sun to the joining of atoms in an expectant mother's body, He created all and holds all together.

And the Scriptures tell us that we're always on His mind. Not one sparrow falls to the ground without our heavenly Father knowing about it. And of how much more worth are we than the birds of the air? The very hairs of our heads are numbered. No, God knows all and is infinitely concerned about me and mine. He is my "*Abba, Father,*" my Daddy in heaven. The more I thought about this, the more confident I became that God had something up His holy sleeve in allowing this to happen.

God was there on Interstate 80 and could have prevented the collision. I knew that. What I didn't know was whether I would ever understand *why* on this side of eternity. But one day, my God would reveal His plan to me. For now, that would have to be enough.

Ever since I had that life-changing experience at sixteen, I have wanted to communicate the God I met to those around me. Finding something so unbelievably awesome left me with a passion to see others possess the treasure also. Because I have sought opportunities to share this great news with others, I have often seen God arrange divine appointments in my everyday affairs—in the super-market, on the playgrounds, wherever—so I could talk to someone about Him.

As a result, I see His touch and guidance in the casual, even mundane, ebb and flow of my life. Even while treading water in a sea of dirty diapers, dirty hands, and dirty laundry, I have known that I am a part of something much bigger than myself. I have a cause to fight for, a mission purposed and issued to me by God, and that is to be an ambassador of God's love. To be one who represents Him to a world that doesn't know Him and often doesn't recognize its need for Him. I believe that my mission field is wherever I am. I am to love others as He has loved me. By His grace I have done that in some small ways. There are no accidents with God, but plenty of opportunities, big and small. The opportunity to love is big. So it wasn't too difficult for me to view Verma Harrison as one whom God had brought into my life to be loved and helped. And I saw her as a person who probably needed large doses of the two.

God, the Good Shepherd, was able and *willing* to help Verma Harrison, and who was in a better position to be used as tools for that than Bill and I if we would let Him? God could infuse her with His Spirit and give her a new life, a new beginning. No, she wouldn't be able to change the past, but He would enable her to make something of her future. That was my hope and the foundation of every prayer for her since the night of the accident.

• • •

Throughout the summer of 1996, I thought about writing to Verma Harrison, but I didn't do it. Mourning for my daughter and my mother consumed me, drained me. In August, I noticed that my hair was falling out. Clumps of shoulder-length hair entangled my fingers whenever I shampooed it. The agony of my sorrow seemed to reverberate throughout every cell of my being. Why shouldn't the root cells of my hair be traumatized too?

I discussed my desire to write to Verma Harrison with Bill, and he encouraged me to do so, although in some ways he was coming from another place. The difference in our approach was evident in our different but equally justifiable viewpoints about reaching out to the woman who had caused the accident. Whereas I said that I wanted to help heal her hurting soul, Bill suggested that we approach her "in the enemy's face." Verma Harrison was not our enemy. Evil itself was. Moreover, if evil is propagated by hatred and revenge—and it is—then he/we wanted no part in it. Bill would choose to forgive and help this woman just to spite the very evil that was behind the scenes of this tragedy. He wanted to choose God and life. And that meant forgiveness.

Forgiving is life-giving not only to the recipient, but also to the giver. If we chose anger, hatred, and revenge, that choice would suck life out of us, and we didn't need any more of *that*. When we succumb to such things, they become our controlling taskmasters, and we become their slaves. Such masters enjoy feasting on our peace of mind and our enjoyment of life. Relationships suffer and even our physical bodies eventually suffer from the putrid sludge of unforgiveness in our minds and emotions.

Forgiveness means that I'm not going to hold the offense against the offender. I am going to be "for" that person, not against. And I am going to "give" the offender, the debtor, the freedom from owing me. In doing so, in giving up my right to punish, I also inevitably give up any hold that the aforementioned taskmasters have on me, and I, too, am set free. As I free the offender from owing me, I, the offended, am freed. I am freed from the inevitable weight that resentment brings. I am free to enjoy. I am free to give and receive love. I am free to grow.

Whether the offender is someone who wasn't sensitive to my feelings and hurt me, or whether it is someone who recklessly drove into my family's car and caused my heart to be ripped out, Jesus is my example. He forgave in the midst of misunderstanding *and* death. While He was dying at the hands of those He had come to save from spiritual darkness, He said, "Father, forgive them, for they know not what they do." Did the Jewish leaders *know* they were condemning a man to death? Yes, they were very conscious that they had delivered this Jesus up to be crucified. Did the Roman soldiers *know* they were executing a man that morning? Did they see the blood oozing from His head as they pressed a thorny hyssop wreath into His flesh? Did they hear the snap of the whip as it descended upon His bloody back, or the sound of metal hitting metal as their mallets drove spikes through His hands and feet, making Him one with the rough beams of a wooden cross? Did they know what they were doing? Yes! They made their choices. So why did Jesus say that they didn't know what they were doing? Because He knew that they didn't really know who He was—the embodiment of the heart of God toward mankind.

And He saw something else that they didn't have the insight to see. He saw the big picture. He saw the war that only spiritual eyes can see: the war of light versus darkness, good versus evil. He was able to look at the source of their evil behavior—Satan, the father of lies. He did not view His executioners as His enemies. He was able to look through them and recognize His true enemy, all the while having compassion on the people who were causing Him unspeakable torment. He was free to choose love because He knew the truth.

Likewise, God has shown me that my enemies are not those who hurt me or cause me harm; my enemies are the dark powers that are continually at work in this world, seeking to destroy the quality of life that God would have me possess. Of course, since I live in a world of imperfect people (which includes me), daily I am faced with interactions that result in my being sinned against or my sinning against someone else. We all know what it's like to hold on to our right to be angry when wronged. For years I struggled with hurt feelings and resentment. I had a *right* to be angry. I had a *right* to be resentful. I had a *right* to retaliate. Or so I thought. In time, however, I realized that God wasn't calling me to be right. He was calling me to *love*.

Let's face it. God has a *right* to wipe out the human race after all we've done against Him and one another. Yet what does He do about our selfish and belligerent acts toward Him and one another? He chooses not to exercise His authority to be right—not yet. Where He could stretch out a pointing, accusing, condemning finger toward any one of us, He chooses to extend an open, welcoming hand that beckons us to grasp it. God's mercy triumphs over His judgment. And once we accept His hand and His forgiveness through Christ, He bids us to love others as He has loved us. This is how He wants us to live, and He will give us the power to do so.

As I thought about all this, I saw that I needed to relinquish my rights to retaliate, even though, from a human perspective, retaliation seemed justifiable. I saw that I was being challenged, by the example of God, to sacrifice my rights for the high calling of love. To withhold myself from meeting this challenge would cause a breach in my relationship with Him. He would always love me—that was not in question. I did not have to earn His love. But to continue to walk with Him, I must do what He says. And besides, it's all for my good anyway. Jesus said, "Whoever desires to save his life will lose it, but whoever loses his life for My sake will find it" (Matt. 16:25 NKJV).

I had learned all this about forgiveness before my walk through the dark valley of death began, and because I had, the flow of God's compassion to me and through me guided my actions when I decided to reach out to Verma Harrison.

. . .

A number of years ago, I began fasting on a regular basis because of the spiritual and physical benefits. God expects His people to fast. Jesus did not say, "*If* you fast." He said, "*When* you fast . . .," and throughout biblical history we find many, many examples of people who fasted. Initially I began to fast and pray when I was in desperate need of help or direction. I was able to get God more in focus and put my anxieties to rest. I had an opportunity to be reminded of how big He is, and my faith grew. Answers to my prayers came as well. Eventually I began to fast and pray weekly for Bill and me and our children. In time I saw other reasons for fasting.

In mid-November, when I finally decided to write to Verma Harrison, I realized that I could write a thousand words to her and they would be meaningless. But God could speak one word to her through me, and she could be changed forever. So I fasted and prayed, seeking God's guidance for just the right words. I fasted for three days while I wrote that first letter to her during my early morning times with God.

On one of those fasting mornings, I was sick to my stomach. Occasionally that happens—as if my stomach is rebelling against not being fed. I was very weak too. *Hey,* I thought. *Hasn't this woman put you through enough? Why do you allow yourself to suffer so for her?* I recognized where those thoughts were coming from—the enemy—and I ignored them. *God knew what He was doing,* I reminded myself. I would follow Him.

Addressing Verma Harrison personally was an emotional feat for me. My mother and my daughter were gone because of this woman. Yet a blanket of peace enveloped me as I sat down to write.

As I started writing, scenes flashed through my mind. I saw a woman crying because she had been hurt by the men in her life. She had trusted them, and they had broken their promises to her. Also, she was crying because of frustration. The woman I saw wanted to do good but was very frustrated because she continually found herself falling far short of what she wanted to be and do. She wanted to teach her children well and to be a good example, but found it impossible to rise above the circumstances of life. I saw that she had inner struggles that continually pulled her down—thoughts that ruled her mind and told her again and again that she would never be anything better than she already was. I believed that God was giving me knowledge of this woman I had never even seen.

Assuming that she was probably scared to death of us, I felt the need for gentleness and simplicity. I wanted her to trust us. I wanted to be her friend.

November 13, 1996

Dear Verma,

You don't know me, but you know of me. My name is Cindy Griffiths. I am the daughter of Janice and Joe Nicolich whose car you hit on June 28, and the mother of Robyn Griffiths, the little girl in the back seat. I have wanted to write to you for some time now.

There are times when I think of you and wonder who you are and what you are like. I wonder how old your kids are and if you enjoy them as much as I do mine. I wonder, too, how it is for you now. But I know so little about you. They told me you have three children of your own. They told me you're my age. They told me some things about your night before the crash, which led to it happening. Other than that I don't know much at all.

Sometimes I wonder if you think of me. Let me tell you a little about myself. I'm thirty-five, soon to be thirty-six in December (the same day, the 12th, as my daughter Robyn would have been 12). I've been married fourteen years to a hard-working self-employed carpenter, Bill. We have six children ages 4-13 yrs. I enjoy gardening and sewing and watching my family devour hot loaves of home-made whole wheat bread. I work out five or six mornings a week and I pray a lot. We have 2 rabbits, 5 guinea pigs (all Robyn's), a bunch of fish, and a new St. Bernard puppy. I home-school all of my children but the oldest (he *was* home-schooled, though).

My days are filled with kids and laundry and what to make for dinner.

Sometimes when I think of you, I wonder if *you* wonder what it's like for my family and me. I'm not really going to describe to you how it's been except to say that it's been like an enormous tidal wave that crashed down on us and many, many others. Yet I am not writing to you today to put guilt on you. I'm writing to let you know that I do not hate you. I do not condemn you, for I have made mistakes, too. I do not wish you to suffer mercilessly, and I do not wish you were dead. I wish, more than anything that this didn't happen—but what good will that do now? I miss my mom and daughter beyond words. I am my mom's only daughter (I have four brothers) and Robyn was my only daughter (with four brothers) till she was seven. She was *sooo* glad to finally have a baby sister. I was very close to both of them.

I don't believe that you woke up on June 27th and decided to go out and harm these people the next morning. I think there were probably many wrong choices that preceded that time. In fact, I would guess that you weren't real happy with your life to begin with—and now this!

Life can be so hard, so unfair, and so cruel at times. We find ourselves wanting what's good and right for our families and ourselves, but pressures from the world around us, as well as desires within us that aren't good, all get in the way. We're left wondering why we just can't make it, get it together, and keep it that way. And so we go from one day to the next trying, struggling, or perhaps not even that; for many it's just hopeless. We can feel so trapped.

If you can relate to any of this, please know that there's hope for you. Do you know why? It's because Jesus Christ lives, and He can set you free and give you a new, clean heart and a new life both here, and after this life. Did you ever notice how everything here dies eventually? Jesus is L-I-F-E. If you put your hand in His, He will put His life in you. And you will know that you will live with Him forever. I've seen many lives changed when people opened their hearts to Him.

Do you know that God loves you very deeply and personally? Jesus said that the very hairs of your head are numbered. God knows all about you. Jesus said that God sees every little sparrow that falls to the ground, and cares for them. If He cares for birds, then how much more does He care for you? For you are worth more than they. He said that God is a *loving* Father who takes care of His own. The problem is, so many are not "His own." So many people keep Him out and never experience the benefits of a relationship with Him. He's a Father, and He's a Friend.

The Lord wants to take you out of the darkness of your own life and give you His life. You might be thinking that it's not possible, even if all that I'm saying *is* true. Maybe you're thinking that you're not good enough. Don't worry—you're not, neither am I, neither is anyone else. Jesus didn't come to save those who have it together. He came to save those who are lost, who can't do it on their own. Really, that means everyone, but some recognize their need for Him, while others are too proud, and blind. So you see, there's great hope and help for those who know they need help and look to God. The Bible says that God is patiently waiting for us to turn to Him so that He may heal us. Oh, how great is His love, how gentle, how strong!

Now, or later when you meet God, you're going to have to give an account of your life. It is worth everything to do it now. If you wait till then, it will be too late. God is going to judge all people. If you don't come to Him now, you will be found guilty then. There's so much to be gained. For Christ was born a sweet, cute little baby for this purpose: to show the world God's heart, and to die up on that cross to take our sin away.

You see, Verma, God really loves you. So much so that Jesus came to suffer and die a death He didn't deserve. And He did it willingly. When He died on that cross, He took the punishment *we* deserve for our wrongs. For every wrong we do is seen by, and actually is against, God. Yes, Jesus took what we had coming to us so we could go free—forgiven. It's like we're before a firing squad for something we did, and we deserve to die, and someone steps in front of us to shield us from the bullets, and he dies instead. And then we're left standing there in shock and disbelief over this action. We find out several days later he's alive and tells us he loves us and would do it all over again if he had to. He tells us the price has been paid. We don't have to suffer.

It's because of His great love that I am not insane today. It is because of His great love that I can write to you now and not hate you. My mother and my sweetie, Robyn, knew Him, too. I know that there is going to be a joyful, awesome end to this story, for I shall see them again at the best party that was ever thrown. God will be throwing *quite* a party when Jesus comes back to bring His friends to heaven. It's gonna be great. No crying, no pain, no mourning, no sickness, no dying, no aging. We're going to be like happy little kids. Happy, nice kids, for there shall be no evil.

I have known, since I was sixteen, that there couldn't be *anything* bigger than Him. He is the Way, the Truth, and the Life. And God is love. I've known His love in many different ways in the past nineteen years. And now I am so glad that I know that His love truly is deeper than my pain, and bigger than any problem. Like I said, this is where my sanity is coming from.

There's a place within me that is wanting very much for you to know Him too. I am praying for you, and so are my friends. I hope that you will allow Him entrance into your heart and life. He loves you and forgives you, but you need to give Him all your sin. He really wants to give you joy that is so strong and so real, a peace that feels so good, and a purpose for living that makes so much sense. There are times in my life I feel so light and free—actually, much of the time. He helps us to look at things and react to people and situations in a new way that is so much better than our own way. He will help you to be what He made you to be in the first place.

Don't think that you need to go to a church to pray, or say memorized prayers. You can talk to Him like a person. He is with you always. He's watching you and is patiently waiting for you to come home to Him where it's safe and warm. Don't be afraid—He understands. You could just say, "Lord, help me. Help me to know You. I need my life changed. I need *me* changed. Take my sin away. Thank You for giving Your life, so I won't have to be eternally condemned and far from You. Please come in and show me how to follow You." It can actually be that simple . . . *if* it's from your heart.

I also want to let you know that the Bible, which is *God's Word*, says, "God causes all things to work together for the good to those who love Him and who are called according to His purpose." That means that He can take all that's happening now and turn it around into something so wonderful, you'll be in awe. It doesn't matter how far we've gotten away from His ways. It doesn't matter how messed up things have become. He is able! He's bigger! Please know that you are not alone. Please let Him in so He can give you the peace you long for. The Bible also says, "Those who hope in Me will not be disappointed (Isa. 49:23 NIV)." He's the only one who will never break His promises to you. You can trust Him. There's so much to be gained.

I hope you will come to know the peace, comfort, love, and purpose that I've known because of Him. He's the only one who can get me through this nightmare. And He's the only one who can get you through yours.

If I can help you to know Him better, or if you wish to write to me at all, my address is . . .

I'm here to help you. Thanks for reading this.

Cindy Griffiths

I made a copy of the letter so I could show it to our kids when they were older, and then I got Verma's address from our lawyer. As I mailed the letter, I wondered if or when I'd get a response. I hoped she'd write.

If the Lord wants us to have a relationship, I thought, *it'll happen. I've done my part. The rest is up to Him.*

CHAPTER 22

GAINING GROUND

(BILL)

There was nothing specific or special about the person of Verma Harrison that impassioned my forgiveness. She could have been Mother Teresa or Genghis Khan and it wouldn't have mattered to me. Unlike Cindy's forgiveness, the passion of my forgiveness drew its flame from anger, not sympathy. I was determined to forgive and love her because this was war.

"Love your enemy" and "bless those who curse you" did not float tenderly and gently through my mind as soft-spoken, biblical encouragements of peace. These verses bore not warmth, but fire. Not comfort, but conviction. They echoed through me like a battle cry, and I held onto them like the handle of a sharpened, bloody, two-edged sword. No way would I let go.

It was an extreme time that conjured extreme emotions. This sword promised me life, and I would not surrender it and my family in a death pool of hate.

Spiritually speaking, love can be violent—more violent than hate. I believe that the most violent act ever committed was by Jesus when He allowed Himself to be crucified. The ripple effect of such violent love sent tidal waves through the heavens. In that light, the most violent act I've ever committed was forgiving Verma Harrison—loving Verma Harrison.

Yet none of this is to take away from the real reason the verses were spoken: the genuine love and mercy from a God who is, first and foremost, compassionate. As time moved forward, the extreme emotion of the tragedy had given way to clear-headed rationality. I finally had overcome blind rage enough to take advantage of past teachings and studies that would now work as my weapons.

Elaine Harwood had once taught that in order to forgive, one had to be forgiving. I needed to separate myself from any personal hate and be gracious, or I would be eaten alive along with so many others who spend the rest of their lives wishing they could get their hands around so-and-so's neck. Recalling another teaching, I knew that life would come from any hatred within me I could kill. Life comes from death. Matches, stars, lightbulbs, car engines—all die to give off life and so would I if I wanted to see life come through this tragedy.

"And forgive us our trespasses as we forgive those who trespass against us" were words and a promise that I also now hold dear. Clearly I am also in need of much mercy, and I want God's flow to continue in my life. Forgiveness is learned by being forgiven. I am loved, and I want to love in return. Love is learned by being loved. I cannot give what I have not received. I've received a lot. My crosshairs are not leveled at Verma Harrison, and I pray they never will be.

CHAPTER 23

HOLIDAYS

(CINDY)

November winds had blown away the last of October's flaming grand finale, and the Thanksgiving and Christmas holidays loomed on the horizon. *Holidays*. I couldn't even bring myself to say the word. Thanksgiving and Christmas without Robyn, without my mother. The bleak late autumn landscape mirrored the emptiness in my heart.

Celebrating Thanksgiving in New Hampshire with Bill and Dorothy Griffiths, Bill's parents, had become a family tradition. In their home, nestled amidst the white birches and towering pines of the Granite State, Bill and Dorothy always had a warm welcome for their two sons and their families. Everything from Dorothy's candled pumpkin centerpieces to the homemade pumpkin and apple pies, swelling up and over their rims, was presented with loving hospitality.

That year, however, as we drove the six hours to their home, it was hard to anticipate the warm glow of the holiday. The sinking feeling that Robyn's absence created within me was very strong.

Robyn had loved visiting Grandma and Grandpa Griffiths, and reminders of her were everywhere. Lake Sunapee and Elkin's Beach on quaint little Lake Pleasant, where she swam in the summer. The slopes near the Griffiths' home in New London, where Grandpa Bill took her and her brothers skiing in the winter, where he taught her to ski. The horses down the road—at Thanksgiving, Robyn would always ask for carrots to feed to them. My nature girl. Sometimes she and I would go for a drive together. We played "Get Lost": I would turn wherever she bid me to, and after a while we'd be "lost" (or almost!) in the gorgeous countryside. Robyn also took advantage of her grandparents' piano, basking in the attention of her captive audience of Grandma, Grandpa, and Great-Grandma.

When we arrived in New London for the first time without Robyn, my heart was saddened at the sight of Bill's brother's girl, Jessica. Jessica is three years younger than Robyn, and both of them always looked forward to spending time together at Grandma's. Robyn was the oldest of the girl cousins and led the way when it came to the younger kids, especially the girls. She loved them, played with them, and helped them tenderly and patiently when needed.

That first night, when I entered the bedroom where the children always slept, my eyes were drawn to the cot under the Norman Rockwell painting where Robyn usually slept. Bill's mom had always put her Raggedy Ann and Andy dolls on the bed for Robyn. Now, Robyn wouldn't be occupying it. *She will never sleep here again*, I thought, and the tears came, but I thanked God, as I had earlier at the dinner table, that Robyn and my mom were with Him. Though she was not with me, I knew she was safe with Him. Once again the Scriptures lifted my heart as I thanked God that my baby was not experiencing the sorrow that I was. She was in a place of everlasting joy.

The year before, Robyn had made Bill a Thanksgiving card. She had drawn a horn of plenty and then written under it, "Dear Dad, 'Give thanks in whatever happens.' First Thessalonians 5:18." Bill wept when he came across this almost prophetic message after the accident. He took it to his office and placed it where he could see it every day.

· · ·

December brought its own searing remembrances and a return to the familiar bottomless realm of sorrow. I still shed tears often, but the gut-wrenching sobs and uncontrollable weeping of June and July did not seize me as frequently. However, I really lost it all again in December, for December 12 was my birthday and Robyn's.

Just the anticipation of that day brought its own sorrow. I do my grocery shopping early Saturday mornings. As I neared the card aisle on the shopping day before our birthday, I was drawn to those sweet daughter cards. Perhaps I should have steered clear of them, but I still loved Robyn and I couldn't *not* get her a card. She would have been twelve. Twelve on 12/12. I'm told that when the age and the month coincide, it's called one's golden birthday. So I bought her a card, which I displayed on the table in the hallway where we put all the birthday cards, announcing the arrival of each family member's special day.

On the morning of the twelfth, the children wrote letters to Robyn. Four-year-old Summer dictated hers to me. Then we bought pink and purple helium balloons, folded up the letters and inserted them, and then inflated the balloons. We tied them with pink ribbon and took them to the cemetery. Once there, the children and I stood in a circle, holding hands as I thanked God for letting us have Robyn for eleven and a half years. For the children's sake, I asked Him to let her read the letters. Then we let the balloons go "up to heaven." I couldn't stop crying.

· · ·

On December 13 and 14, I danced in the Christmas program at my mother's church. They had phoned me in October and asked if I would participate. The program, they said, would be dedicated to my mom and Robyn. I told them I would be honored to participate.

However, in the evening after the first show, I was a mess. That night the forty-minute drive home was horrible. I was alone and so lonely. In the past, Robyn and/or my mother always attended such events with me. The three of us loved local holiday shows and Broadway performances. That night, without them, I was lost and bereft.

Halfway home, I exited off the parkway and stopped at the EAB Plaza in Uniondale. Two years ago, in December of 1994, Robyn and I had danced here to a piece of music performed by my mother's church choir (in which she sang). Everything was bedecked in Christmas adornment, and the choir sounded incredible. I remember thinking that no choir of angels could have sounded more beautiful. They sang, and we danced for the festive onlookers.

I pulled into the parking lot and checked my watch. It was late. The doors were still open, but a security guard told me they were locking up. I stood there not knowing what to do. I should say okay and leave, but I couldn't. Then, somehow, the words rolled out . . . I'd lost my mother and daughter in a car accident and I had some memories of being with them here, and could I please just sit inside for a few minutes? The man looked sympathetic albeit confused, then stepped aside to let me pass.

Once within, I went over to the atrium, where there was a low stone wall. I sat on it and peered into the almost empty lobby, my eyes locking on places where I could visualize scenes from that night. I could imagine the choir, with my mom standing in her place. And I remembered Robyn and me moving around the floor in front of them.

All at once, the tears came.

There were still some people around, heading for the doors. I covered my face with my hands and tried to weep silently.

Then I sensed a presence beside me. The security guard sat down next to me. "Are you all right?" he asked.

I proceeded to give him a three-minute version of how I had come to be there, sharing my deep pain with this total stranger. *Out of the abundance of the heart the mouth speaks,* I thought. *I'm just so full of this grief sometimes, why should I be surprised when it leaks out to a total stranger? This is too big for me. There really is no containing it.*

I drove home that night weary from the emotions and wondering whether it was wise for me to put myself through that kind of ordeal. Yet in the days ahead I realized that going there that night had closed a door for me. Since the accident, whenever I'd pass that plaza, the memory of that Christmas dance had stabbed me like a knife. Now, however, after deliberately walking down memory lane on that cold December night and allowing my emotions to surface, I could drive past the place and not feel such deep pain. The memories made me sad, but the pain was lessened.

Another haunting task that December was shopping for Christmas gifts. I could not give anything to Robyn, and yet I did not want to stop giving to her. I kept seeing things in the stores that I knew she would like. How I wanted to buy her something. So, when I saw an ad for a charitable organization looking for Christmas gifts for children, I knew I had found an answer to prayer. The kids and I went shopping and picked out several gifts for a girl Robyn's age (donors could choose the age bracket they desired to give to), and we selected gifts that Robyn would have enjoyed. We boxed them up (everything had to fit in a shoebox) and sent the package to the address listed in the ad. I requested that our gifts be sent to war-torn Yugoslavia, since that is where my parents' people are from, and I had been praying for the nation and especially its children.

. . .

Several days before Christmas, I learned that I was pregnant again. I was sure that this partly accounted for the depth of emotion I had experienced lately. I decided I would wait until Christmas morning to tell Bill. I wrote a note, as if from the unseen family member, to Bill. I wrapped it up in a box and placed it under the tree. Then I saved it as the last gift to be opened. When Bill read the message, he looked at me and, with love in his eyes, asked, "Really?" I just nodded, and he pulled me close and held me awhile.

I was determined to make the Christmas holiday colorful, flavorful, and memorable for the family. I wondered whether we'd all make it together for the next one. But it was during this holiday season that I finally began to grieve over the loss of my mother. Before then, I was unable to focus on anything but Robyn; there seemed to be no room in my soul for anything else. Oh, I had missed my mother, but it was mostly because I wanted to cry on her shoulder because Robyn had been ripped out of my life. I wanted my "mommy." But it was Christmastime when the waves of grief for my mother smashed down upon me and left me feeling like a little girl lost on a vast beach.

Bill was so good to me through all of this. Many times, when my emotions rose up from deep, deep within and needed to be vented, he'd just put his arms around me and hold me till I stopped crying. But I did learn that I couldn't *always* tell him about the things that happened during the day that reminded me of Robyn. There were so many things, and by sharing them with him, expecting him to listen at every turn, I saw that I was adding to the rawness of *his* pain. If I felt the need for a real flesh-and-bones connection, but didn't want to drag my hurting husband down with me, I sometimes called a friend. Most of the time, I spoke to God alone.

CHAPTER 24

My Mother, My Friend

(Cindy)

Grieving for my child had left no room for grieving for my mother. Mentally I understood that my mother was gone, too, but I could not feel sorrow for her loss. If I were to describe the waves of grief for my mother as being as tall as the maple tree in my front yard, then the waves of grief for Robyn reached up into space. The grief for my baby simply overpowered everything else. I didn't let myself feel guilty about it; I just figured I had no control over it. And of course, I didn't.

For as long as I can remember, Mom and I had been friends. I was her first and only daughter, coming along after she and Dad had three boys, my brothers Joe, Rob, and Ray. Then Scott came after me. Being the only girl in the midst of four very active boys caused Mom and me to bond in a special way. She once told me, after I had children of my own, that she knew it was rough for me as a child, since I was the only girl. She felt at times that I needed someone on my side. But I'm sure that much of our closeness developed simply because we were mother and daughter.

The earliest memory I have is just a snapshot image in my mind. I see the dashboard of a car with streetlights above it. In the lower half of this image, I see my arms clothed in a fuzzy pink jacket, and my arms are resting on my mother's coat sleeves. I'm on her lap, we are going somewhere, and I feel safe with my mother's arms around me. (Actually we were going to a hospital because I had pneumonia and was running a high fever. I was two.)

Throughout my life I have felt my mother's comforting arms around me. Many more times, her kindness and friendship hugged my heart.

From the time I was a little girl, she made me feel that I was important to her. When I joined the Girl Scouts, for example, she joined with me, making time to become a Girl Scout leader. I suppose the Scouting experience would have been fun anyway, but my mother's being there certainly fostered a "Mom and me" mentality in my impressionable soul and gave us countless opportunities to laugh and learn together.

I can remember her encouraging me to earn those badges, and I earned quite a few as a Junior Girl Scout. Unfortunately, some of the other girls just "knew" that my mother gave the badges to me without my doing the work. But Mom and I knew better. She never let me cut any corners when it came to fulfilling the necessary requirements.

My mother loved kids and loved to be with them. Maybe that was because she was so much of a kid herself. She could relate to their humor and horseplay. Mom was also intelligent and could share information in an interesting manner, thus becoming the teacher-guide, exercising her authority when necessary. Perhaps it had to do with her being the oldest of four children, but my mother was a natural leader.

She'd get the girls feeling comfortable with her at a campfire gathering by being silly and having fun and singing our songs, and then she'd break out the flashlight and star charts and enthrall us all with her talks about the night sky. The other girls benefited from her leadership, knowledge, humor, and friendship, but I was privileged to be her daughter, and therefore a constant recipient of all this and more.

In the ebb and flow of life, children learn so much from the examples of the adults around them. I've heard it said that more is caught than taught. Children learn more from what we do than from what we say. My mother often said that she loved me, but her being there in so many ways communicated her love to my heart more than anything else.

When I reached my teen years, my mother became my sounding board on many occasions. While I began to see, as all children eventually do with their parents, that she wasn't the perfect angel of my early years, I always *knew* that she loved me. How many times she would listen to me describing, in painstaking detail, the sequences of my gymnastic routines, wanting her to understand precisely what I was seeing in my mind and wanting her to feel the music of my floor routines the way I felt them. She might have had a genuine interest at times, but in retrospect, I think the truth is that she had a genuine interest in me as a person and as her daughter.

Maybe she had thoughts like the ones I so often had for Robyn and still do for Summer. Thoughts like, *Wow! This is my daughter. I'm her mother. We are gifts to one each other. I will listen. And not just listen. I will try to hear.* (Of course, these heart thoughts hold true for my sons as well.) But whatever my mother's thoughts were, she made me feel valuable.

Then came the ups and downs of my romantic teenage heart. Throughout those years, my mother was there to try to help. I didn't confide in her as I did my best girlfriend, but when I needed her, she listened and tried to make sense of my emotions. Sometimes just hearing ourselves voice our problems is an aid in itself. It can help us to gain perspective and decide which thoughts are worth holding onto and which to discard permanently.

Years after I had the life-changing experience at sixteen, my mother told me that she initially thought it was some kind of fad I was going through. Usually, I'd be out with my friends on weekend evenings, but now, instead of looking for feel-good experiences through typical teenage routes, I had a deep desire to know this God, this Person, who had touched the deepest part of me with His love. Frequently my mother found me alone in my room with a Bible and guitar. She didn't understand what was happening to me, and she wondered why I wasn't out with my friends more. Not that I had dropped my friends. We'd still talk in school, but when it came to after-school activities, I wasn't interested in drinking parties and other things that seemed to be fun to them. I tried to help my mother understand why I felt the way I did, why I so enjoyed the peace and love that God's presence was bringing to my emotional teenage heart. I'm not sure that I succeeded at that point, but I know she listened.

Years later, she told me that my growing interest in spiritual matters served as a catalyst to heighten her own inquisitiveness and eventually helped her to reach out and take the hand of God as I had.

• • •

Because Mom was very emotional, she was a crier: tears of sorrow, tears of sadness, tears of gladness, tears of joy. She would cry over a sad movie. But her eyes would also glisten over the happy ending to a movie or a beautiful ice-skating performance.

The giving of thanks was not a daily ritual at our dinner table, but seemed to be saved for special occasions such as religious holidays. Yet my mother would always choke up at those moments, barely able to verbally express what her heart contained, for she would not give thanks for food alone, but for the blessings of family and togetherness.

She would cry when we sang patriotic songs like "The Battle Hymn of the Republic" and "The Star-Spangled Banner" and especially "America the Beautiful" on the long drives to a family camping vacation. When we watched Neil Armstrong walk on the moon, Mom's eyes glistened. When I was younger, I didn't understand this tendency. Now I do. As I sing those patriotic songs with my children, especially with Robyn, who loved to sing, I find that I, too, can be teary. I, too, must occasionally pause to center myself so my voice doesn't crack while I'm recounting a historic tale to the children as I read aloud to them. I think I understand now why my mother expressed such emotion over these things.

I remember her tears when I tried on a wedding dress "just to get an idea of the style" (we were planning on sewing one). Then there were her tears at the wedding and at the birth of each of our children.

One of my last memories of my mother's "emotional sparkling eyes" was at a Christmas service at our church. Robyn, then nine, and I were doing an interpretive dance, which I had choreographed for the two of us. We danced to a song about the birth of Christ—a sweet song taken from a children's animated video. At one point, while Robyn and I moved with the gentle cadence of the music, I looked straight ahead at those who were watching us. There was my mom sitting in the front row, directly in front of us, her face looking almost troubled. I knew it was because she was trying not to show her emotions. She was trying to hide what was welling up inside her. But her wet cheeks and furrowed brow gave it away, even better than her words did later on when we were alone together.

. . .

In April 1996, just two months before the accident, my niece Aspen flew to New York from Utah to spend time with the family here. One day we went to Jones Beach. It was too cool for swimming, but it was an unusually warm early spring day, and Aspen and our children and my brother Scott's kids had a great time together, Rollerblading in some unused tennis courts and playing in the playground. My mom and dad were enjoying the grandkids, and Dad was busy with his camera, as usual.

Later, when we strolled along the boardwalk, I put my arm through my mom's, as I often did. As we walked, I was aware of the warmth of the sunshine on my face and the gentle breeze lifting my hair. Most of all, I was aware of the love I shared with my mother. Thinking about our relationship, I was overcome with the goodness of the Creator for letting me have her for my mom. As my heart swelled with gratitude, I burst out in a song in praise to Him. I don't remember which song it was, but I do remember my mother singing with me—of one mind and one spirit.

We are all gifts to one another. At least our lives are meant to be, by a loving and wise Designer. Yet too often the gift of who we are is obscured. In some people, we may see a talent or talents, and thereby place a measure of worth on them according to their ability. But whether one has unique talents or not, all of us have thorns in personality that others must accept and look past in order to appreciate the fragrance of our worth. My mother was not perfect—no one is. But her life was a gift to all who knew her, and I have been blessed to be her daughter.

. . .

About two or three weeks prior to their trip west, Mom called me to ask if I'd be her guest at a mother-daughter Girl Scout dinner. I chuckled and asked, "Don't you think I'm a little old for that? I retired my uniforms a long time ago."

I could hear the smile in her voice as she told me she wanted me to join her anyway. I thought about all the things I needed to do that evening at home, but gave in to the quiet thought that said, *It's good to be with Mom.* Bill was working, so my dad stayed with the kids while Mom and I went to the Girl Scout dinner.

During the course of the dinner, my mind periodically wandered to all those fun things I was missing at home. Like doing the laundry, cleaning up a dirty kitchen, and putting children, who'd insist they weren't tired, to bed. Between home-schooling three children and keeping tabs on three preschoolers, I had to pace myself or I'd burn out. I needed to be careful about how much time I spent away from the roost. So I was pondering those sundry tasks when that thought came again, accompanied by a feeling of well-being: *It's good to be with Mom.*

For the remainder of the evening, I set my mind to enjoying our time together. Several weeks later, I realized that that night was our last mother-daughter date.

What a treasure I had in my mother. What a treasure I had been parted from—at least for a while. My mother, Janice Nicolich. Empathizer, joker, family psychologist, star gazer, admirer of beauty, teacher, eternal student, conversationalist, reader, grandma, family hub, Girl Scout, Tupperware lady, choir member, camper, hugger, crier, laugher, motorcycle rider (okay, passenger), personal cheerleader, optimist, beholder of God, philanthropist, kindred spirit, my labor attendant, my sister, my friend, my *mother.*

CHAPTER 25

SPECIAL DELIVERY

(CINDY)

I'd gotten used to *not* seeing a letter from Verma Harrison in my mailbox. Every day I thought, *Maybe today*. Knowing how long it had taken me to finally sit down and pen a letter to her, I figured she must have a kaleidoscope of thoughts and emotions to sort through before she could put a stamp on the envelope that bore my name (if, in fact, there was even going to be one). Yet each day I hoped. And each day I prayed for her.

Then, the third week of January, on a Saturday morning, I stopped at the post office after finishing my weekly grocery shopping. And there, amid the bills and junk mail, was a letter with Verma Harrison's name in the return address. Actually it was more than a letter. It was a large manila envelope.

Immediately my heart started beating double time. I couldn't wait to get home to open it. I wasn't going to read it in the car. No, I was not going to rush. It was too important. This was big, very big. I wanted to be at home where Bill was, and I wanted privacy when I opened Verma Harrison's letter.

I backed the Suburban into the driveway and hurried into the kitchen. I called to the boys to unload the groceries and showed Bill the envelope. He took a breath and exhaled slowly, as if to say, "This is it." He didn't read it with me, though. It was too hard for him. He would let me read it and then fill him in later.

Then I went to the place where everyone goes for privacy—the bathroom. I locked the door. My heart was pounding, but I felt chilled. *Lord, be with me,* I prayed. My hands trembled as I opened the envelope and pulled out a many-paged, handwritten letter, a Christian news publication titled *Hosanna! Magazine,* a pamphlet describing a Christ-centered rehab program called Overcomers Outreach, and eight-by-ten-inch photographs of Verma Harrison and her family.

The pictures shocked me. I wasn't expecting photos. Her older boy, twelve like Robyn would have been, was in his football uniform. The younger two, a girl and a boy, wore traditional Native American garb. Her daughter was beautiful—*like an Indian princess,* I thought.

And then I saw *her.* My eyes locked on the woman through whom it all had happened. I looked at her for a long time. *Who are you?* I wondered. My eyes welled up with tears.

I turned my attention to her twenty-six-page letter. I continued to tremble as I read it. She included much information about her childhood, which I've omitted to protect her privacy, but here are parts of that letter:

11-29-96

Dear Mrs. Griffiths and Family,

   Ya "ateeh." It is well.

   I have prayed for this day when I would be given the opportunity to ask you and your family for your forgiveness. I'm afraid in doing this Mrs. Griffiths. I can't even begin to imagine what your lives are like now! I wish I could take that morning back!

I think of you all every moment of my life now. I wonder all the time how your family is handling all this, and how you must despise me. I wouldn't blame you. I'm even more ashamed than before.

Please hold your father and family, even gather them and read them this. Please know that I *never* meant to hurt anyone! This is most difficult for me . . . every day is a struggle. Forgive me. I'm not sure, legally, what I'm not supposed to say or write—but I'm going to speak from my heart.

I'm terrified! I hate myself for allowing such a tragedy. I wanted to end my life. It still crosses my mind on the most difficult days . . . I wonder now, often times, if it's still worth living. Time and again, I just want to disappear, die. If I do, what will happen to my babies? Who's going to take care of them for me? Who's going to kiss them goodnight? . . . Mrs. Griffiths, you can't do this with Robyn any more . . . Why, why did I survive? Do I deserve to live? . . .

What will happen to me? What's going to happen to my children? What have I done? What do I do? What's left for everyone whose lives are permanently altered?

Yes, it has been a nightmare. For the first three days after the accident, I kept hoping I'd wake up any minute and find it to be only a dream. How I wish it was! You're right, Mrs. Griffiths. What good will that do now? Everyone and everything involving this whole circumstance is on my mind and pierces my heart tremendously EVERY MOMENT OF EVERY DAY!

I feel even more worthless than before. You and your family are with me all the time. Wherever I go, whatever I do, in everyone I see. I often wonder what your mother and baby were like . . . All the time, Mrs. Griffiths . . . I think about them all the time.

How your family must be missing them, I'm sorry. Especially now with the holidays upon us. Only "Shi Diyin" (my Holy One) knows how my heart goes out to you. Please forgive me again . . .

Mrs. Griffiths, you have given me the greatest gift with your act of showing God's love through your forgiveness. This is a gift that's long been needed in my life. Yes, God has made Himself real to me through your words of forgiveness, love, and hope. He answered all my questions in EVERY WORD you wrote! My burden was unbelievably heavier than ever until I received your letter. Before that, I was still struggling with my belief and faith in my Creator . . .

In your letter, you stated you knew Christ since you were sixteen. Wow, that's a very long time. You sound so gentle, loving, accepting, and kind. You brought I John 2:5 to reality for me. [First John 2:5 states, "But whoever keeps His word, in him the love of God has truly been perfected."] God's love is complete in you. How else could it be? Thank you for giving it to me . . . Mrs. Griffiths, *with all my heart—* through the name of our Lord Jesus Christ I'm telling you—I never meant to hurt your family or anyone else! I'm truly sorry!

Sometimes I still wish it was me whose breath was taken, and not your loved ones. Then I think of where I *know* I would've ended up if I did. My burden is lightened to know your Robyn and mother knew our Maker.

Your letter of forgiveness solidified my faith and belief. I know it's God's calling that I was kept alive to fulfill a purpose, but what? Whatever it may be, I'm listening and willing. Our Creator is truly within you, Mrs. Griffiths. I thank Him constantly for giving me this opportunity to let you know that I do care and that I'm truly sorry. How could I have let this happen? If only . . .

I will now tell you about myself and why I had wandered away from God's teachings up to now . . .

I'm a member of the Navajo (Dine) Tribe from the Southwest. I'm thirty years old and am a mother to three children, Josiah, 12, Tsisi, 7, and Braden, 5 . . .

I'm a full-time student at the Laramie County Community College. Studying Computer Technology and hope to be graduating in May. I'm also a silversmith . . . I do beadwork . . . I've always enjoyed creating my own designs. In a way, it helped me feel worth and besides it's been a source of income since I was 6-7 years old. I picked it up from my mother . . .

My long-term goal was to start or open up a shop with Native American Arts here in Cheyenne. That was the reason why I took computer tech courses, so I could keep books . . .

I worked *very hard* (maybe too hard), these last few years to try and restore unity and stability [to her family, which had experienced the split of a divorce]. A healthy, loving family environment was what I wanted to achieve. In the long process, it became too overwhelming for me. It seemed like the more I made the effort, the worse I became. My work, single-parenting, money shortages, stress, loneliness, etc. . . . I went under . . . But instead of reaching out for help, I reached for the bottle.

I became a quiet drunk, sipping away the struggles, pain, anxiety, anger, resentments, bad memories, loneliness, paranoia—you name it, I had it! I drank to numb my feelings and fear. In this process, I managed to keep up with everything—school meetings, parenting classes, games, presentations for different organizations such as United Way, and other activities. I didn't realize exactly when my addiction took over.

In all my life there really wasn't a time I reached out to anyone. Until two days after this accident—I turned to God.

I was in a strange, cold place—my jail cell—dressed in stinky, orange, over-sized clothing with no shoes. What I had walked away from—I had become. How? Why? What now? Who's going to help me? Who cares enough?

When I talked to God that day (6-30-96) I was still very angry. I said to him, "Here you go again, hurting me. When are you going to stop? What are you trying to do to me? What have I ever really done to deserve all this? (The pain all my life through) When is it going to stop?" . . .

It seems I was born into a life of despair—no love—no hope— no care. I always wished I could be someone else, somewhere else or even nonexistent! Through it all though, I never intended for lives to be lost because of my hardships. How I wish I could turn back time or even extinguish my existence.

My struggle has become even more difficult now, but I no longer think too much about ending my existence. Mrs. Griffiths, God has made Himself REAL to me through you! You are truly His child. I glorify His Name on account of receiving His and your gift. The gift of forgiveness. I felt ashamed not being able to forgive my family for their wrongs against me and here you are forgiving me through the love of Christ . . .

Faith and obedience—they have given me the strength I need to overcome sin and temptation—to live a new and more abundant life. I know I must live in this world and yet live apart with my Creator. My inner life must be lived apart from the world. I understand now all successful living arises from this inner life. Through the love of God, you have helped me find that secret place of peace . . .

My Eternal God is my only refuge now. I retire into my own place of meditation to get away from my sense of failure, my weaknesses, and shortcomings. I remain there until the immensity of His Spirit envelops mine and it loses its smallness and weakness and comes into harmony again with His. That's how I lose my limitations now. God's love is getting me through.

I carry your letter with me wherever I go, Mrs. Griffiths, because I know it's God's words . . . He's got my attention. I wish always it could've been another way, but He knew I had become very hard-hearted as the years went by . . .

I'm in counseling twice a week with very nice Christian counselors . . . They're available to me twenty-four hours a day. They have been very loving towards my family and me. I've come to love them back . . . I'm studying the women of the Bible, in hopes I can utilize my knowledge to help single parents. Preferably, Native American women and children, since I know what issues they face . . .

Please pray for us. I've also included an "Overcomer" booklet to have you see how God can restore the hopeless through this program. It's amazing! I've heard some awesome reports. We fellowship every Friday night. I'm blessed more and more each time. My counselors are beautiful people. They, too, are truly God's people. I have shared my letter with them, yours as well. I tell you, I cried so hard [when she received my letter], I cried for days. So great is His love!

I believe now that all our life is a preparation for something better to come . . . His plans work out in the fullness of time. God's miracle-working power is becoming manifest in my life, I wish I knew this beauty long ago! There's nothing or no one who's going to take my precious gift—my Jesus—from me. My longing has been satiated, and I tried everything else. There's nothing like having God's strength in me, He's my life.

I've always felt I was alone—from the beginning of my life to now. But I know now He's never left me. I was the one who had stayed away from Him, but only because my innocence and faith were stolen from me by the very people I loved. Trust has never been a part of my life . . .

With all the fears, shame, guilt, embarrassment and the teaching of showing weakness when you reach out for help—all this combined—ruined me. [As a Native American woman, she had been taught that her dignity would be spoiled if she talked about personal struggles.] It was very difficult for me to go back and take a look at my life. There's so much pain I covered up. So much that was never resolved. Too much. I praise God for giving me my second chance at life. Only He knows what that will bring me . . .

What have I done? The opposite of what I'd always dreamed and hoped for. In a lot of ways I feel my life is over. My humanity tells me it's not worth trying any more—that I'll be put away for life, that I have no more value—but my spirit tells me different. God tells me different. You told me different. I'm sorry, Mrs. Griffiths, I wish I could take everything back. I wish I could have met you and be writing to you under different circumstances. I've robbed your family, my children, and myself. I'm sorry . . .

No matter what happens, I will always treasure our exchange. It's a testimony . . .

I hope that you come to understand and know me better by having read my correspondence. I know I've taken a long time, but I've prayed every time I sat down to write. I began responding a week after I received your letter. Today is the 3rd of January. (Now I need to rewrite.) I return to school on 1-6-97 and so do my babies . . .

I don't know what the outcome of all this will be, but the greatest out of all is this—I finally know God for who He really is!

If you can share more scriptures, please write. I do need you. I don't have much to offer, I've always been poor—so I know that not only money can bring contentment—but I offer my care, love, respect, and heart to you in the name of our Lord Jesus Christ. May our Creator bless and comfort you, and continue working in your lives as He so obviously has been.

In His precious name I'll conclude my letter here.

Sincerely through Jesus
Christ's Name and Love,
Shiwonaji
Verma J. Harrison

. . .

I read her letter and reread it. I read it with caution because I didn't want to believe something simply because it was what I *wanted* to see and hear. I wanted truth.

Her account of her personal history certainly confirmed what my instincts had been telling me about her life and situation. She seemed to have some biblical understanding and appeared to be in some kind of Christian-based recovery program. People of faith were reaching out to her, and she was willing to receive their help. It was almost too good to be true.

In what she wrote and what she left unwritten, between the lines, I sensed her pain over what she'd done to us. I tried to put myself in her place. What do you say to the family you've devastated permanently? How do you say, "I'm sorry for killing your mother and your daughter"? I think that the remorse would be beyond words, just as there have not been words enough to console us.

Time would tell if Verma Harrison would allow God to help her. He, as the Master Sculptor, could take any old lump of clay and make it into a masterpiece. But was she really as willing as she seemed to be? That would be the key.

One thing was for sure. I was going to write back. I was going to be her friend, whether or not she was going to change. For Jesus' sake, for my mom's and Robyn's sakes, I was going to be her friend.

Soon after we received the letter from Verma Harrison, we shared it with our family, as she requested. No one believed either her remorse or her desire to change. They were disgusted. Some felt she was trying to pull my heartstrings in an attempt to win my compassion. They were too hurt and angry to care anything about her. I understood. If God were not in my life, I don't think I would have cared either. I continued to pray for their peace.

• • •

Hearing from Verma Harrison was not the only surprise I received that first month of 1997. And this time, the news was not good. I started having problems with the pregnancy, and a week later, on January 28, I miscarried.

In December, when I had discovered that I was pregnant, I thought, *God has taken (or allowed to be taken) away, and now He is giving.* Not to replace Robyn. That would be impossible. But perhaps to comfort us and help heal us somehow. When I miscarried, I felt that I'd walked into a brick wall. I couldn't believe it. After losing so much, why this?

I had miscarried a pregnancy in October of 1995 too. That time, I had been very ill with some kind of flu and ran a temperature of 103 for three days. This time, however, I had not been sick. I was told that the toll of the trauma of grief on my body could have been too much to maintain the proper balanced environment for the baby. But no one really knows for sure. I just hope that Robyn and my mom have now been united with these two souls where they are. I believe they have.

CHAPTER 26

LIKE SHEEP

(BILL)

While pondering our decision to forgive Verma Harrison, I am reminded of a lesson I learned from a most unlikely teacher.

I had heard so many references to God as a shepherd and to people as sheep that one day I decided to get myself one—a sheep, that is, not a shepherd. The fact that we were sharing a rented house on a one-third-acre lot in suburban Long Island was not enough to deter me.

Cindy was game but suggested I call city hall to make sure I wasn't breaking any laws. I called.

"Are there any ordinances against having a pet sheep in Glen Cove?" I asked.

"A pet . . . sheep?"

"Yes."

"Hmm, hold on."

I waited and waited and waited.

"Sir?"

"Yes?"

"There are no records of anyone ever having a pet sheep in Glen Cove, but the consensus around here is that if your neighbors complain, you'll have to get rid of it."

That afternoon my friend Kevin returned from the country with a fuzzy little lamb. We promptly named him Matthew, not Matt. We agreed that nicknames would be inappropriate for our distinguished guest, although if we knew what his fleece would eventually look like, "Matt" might have been more descriptive.

Over the next couple of weeks Matthew grew so fast that we could practically hear him grow. And I walked him every day. Elizabeth didn't like to leave the property, but Matthew was up for anything. I went everywhere with him: through the neighborhood, the parks, the beach, and even the middle of downtown Glen Cove. The whole time Matthew never left my heels. If I took a step to the left, he took a step to the left. If I left the sidewalk to step around a tree, so would he. And nothing distracted him. Not dog, cat, or screeching car (and there were quite a few of them as we walked by) could derail Matthew's focus.

Yes, Matthew attracted a lot of attention.

"Hey," someone would yell from across a busy street of rubbernecking traffic. "What *is* that thing?"

"It's a sheepdog," I would usually say.

"No kidding. Looks just like a real sheep," he would often reply.

"That's why they call it a sheepdog," I would tell him and then continue on as he stared.

The stories and analogies I could tell you about Matthew are many. The sheep story that I find the most interesting began on one of our walks through town.

"Is that what I think it is?" said a policeman out the window of his patrol car.

"Sure is."

"You can't walk through the streets with a sheep."

I was a little surprised because I had encountered the police on numerous other occasions, always favorably. Maybe the problem was that Matthew had grown to two hundred pounds. "Actually I did get permission from city hall," I said, stretching the truth.

The cop frowned. "Well, I want to see it on a leash."

"He doesn't need a leash," I argued.

"I said . . . I want it on a leash," he said, emphasizing every word.

"Fine."

The next day Matthew was fitted with a collar and leash. His neck was so thick that only the largest collar would work, and the leash was twelve feet long. I felt sad while putting it on him. I was proud of the fact he didn't need it, but I didn't want him to end up in the dog pound or be slapped with a violation. For his part, he didn't seem to mind. While I was trying to secure the clasp under his dense wool, his horizontal pupils stared blankly straight into space. But when we started to walk, his reaction was one I'll never forget.

Instead of walking at my heels as he had done every other time out, he walked at the length of the leash. He wasn't resisting, still walking as he always had, but now twelve feet behind me. Strange. After about a block, I stopped and took the leash off and walked. Matthew was back. Right there. He didn't even think about it. I put the leash back on . . . twelve feet back.

"What is this?" I said to Matthew. "What is this?" I said to God.

Having owned many dogs, I can tell you that they behave much differently on walks. A dog always has his nose, ears, and eyes fully engaged. Without getting into the world of distractions that awaits the attention-deficit hyperactive canine—an animal I can easily relate to—the sheep is interested only in following, and eating if stopped long enough for it to realize there's grass under its feet. That is, until it is leashed. What did this leash represent?

The only answer I could think of was, the law.

After not being able to shake thinking about the sheep's strange behavior, I considered the first thing the serpent wanted Eve to do in their infamous conversation was look at the law. The craftiest beast of the field was an expert with the law—and, indeed, the first lawyer—and had to get Eve to *look at the law*. He had to get her to take her eyes off God and onto the law. That proved to be the beginning of the end.

This set of instructions wrapped around Matthew's neck would teach him what "to do" and what "not to do." He would no longer be able to stop or stray without a painful reminder that he was behaving incorrectly. By necessity, he would have to pay strict attention to this new enforced artificial conscience or risk the consequences. So much for a sheep to think about. Before, he had to watch only what I was doing and where I was going, something he never tired of and appeared to enjoy. Now, he had to calculate my movements with the movements of his new focus—the leash. Unlike a dog, a sheep isn't very good at calculating anything.

Clearly he was following the leash where he had once followed me. Or keeping with the analogy, he was following the law. In this shepherd-sheep relationship I had with Matthew, the leash, or the law, had put a distance between us. Before he was put on the leash, he had been doing everything he was supposed to do and excelled; now he was still behaving, but the magic was gone.

This little analogy eventually proved helpful to me in forgiving

Verma Harrison. How? I'm sorry, but to explain this I might sound a bit preachy.

I love how Jesus slammed the Pharisees for heaping religious laws upon the people, and how He beckoned those who were weary and heavy laden from the law to take His yoke upon themselves, for His yoke is easy and His burden is light. In the Sermon on the Mount, Jesus revealed to those who would seek to be holy by keeping the law how far short they were of their goals by disclosing high standards beyond their comprehension. Even the most stringently legalistic of them would be doomed miserably to failure.

The apostle Paul took four chapters in the heart of the book of Romans to detail the dynamics of the law and its effect on grace, sin, and our relationship with God. A former Pharisee and master of the law, the now enlightened Paul wrote such brow-furrowing statements as these: "The Law came in that the transgression might increase" (Rom. 5:20), and, "Apart from the Law sin is dead" (Rom. 7:8). And then in a verse that goes back to that fatal conversation in the Garden of Eden, Paul said sin is "*aroused* by the Law" (Rom. 7:5).

Jesus said that love would fulfill the law, but just as the leash, the law requires only obedience. Take love out of the equation, and the only motivations I have left to keep the law are based on pride, guilt, or fear—or a combo of the three. And since my ability to keep the law is inadequate, the conviction of failure in my life often translates into anger toward others who break the law. The law brings a demand for me to condemn the condemner. I find it difficult, if not impossible, to focus on the law without becoming critical of myself and others. And God's advice toward criticism comes with a warning: judge not, lest you be judged, and whatever you measure out will be measured against you. My tendency is to find fault with anyone who is pointing out my shortcomings. And my own pointing fingers require constant self-justification. My self-justification feels as if I'm trying to hold water in my bare hands, and to be at all successful, I need to be tremendously shortsighted because my leaky hands feed guilt and fear. This vicious cycle can be crushing and confusing.

Consequently, when my eyes are on God, I can forgive more easily than when my eyes are on the law. Without the law that cries out for justice, I can forgive because I *see* God forgiving. Or in sheep terms, I forgive because I'm following a shepherd who is forgiving.

Of course, this analogy speaks more highly of Cindy than of me. Upon hearing that a drunk driver was involved in the accident, she immediately saw God forgiving, and she followed like an unleashed lamb. When the crisis was suddenly upon us, her eyes were sensitive to follow after compassion and mercy. While I, too, saw God loving and forgiving Verma, the object closer to my view was a shotgun.

Why?

I don't believe that it's as simple as she is who she is and I am who I am. Cindy isn't legalistic, but her devotional life leaves mine in the dust. She spends more time exercising her spiritual muscles. Like the physical, the spiritual side of us is strengthened with repetitive movements against resistance. The reps are time spent reading the Scriptures, praying, worshiping, and getting together with others who are also exercising. The resistance is the constant competition with time and energy. She was in shape, spiritually ready, but I wasn't.

My eye immediately defaulted to the law. "Thou shalt not kill." "An eye for an eye." If not for screaming out to God (prayer), I might still be looking at the law, feeding fuel to hate, and seeing no alternative to punishment.

Forgiveness is love and a key that unlocks the chains. Forgiveness puts the law back where it belongs—behind God—so that when we look for it, we see God instead. And as I mentioned, to see God's love and forgiveness in my own life makes it easier to forgive others.

Unlike dogs, sheep are slow to recognize their shepherd upon first sight. Matthew would always greet me with a blank stare before eventually becoming very excited. It took him a while to remember that I was the guy who brought him his food and water and played with him. Maybe that is why worship services usually get off to a slow start and build. Worship tends to pry our eyes off the law and onto God.

Jesus said, "Follow Me." He said that He does only what He *sees* the Father doing. Cindy and I see the Father forgiving.

PART 5

THE ROAD TO FORGIVENESS

CHAPTER 27

THE ROAD WIDENS

(CINDY)

Each season brought its own host of Robyn and Mom memories. That first winter it was ice-skating, one of Robyn's favorite activities. How many times had I skated around the rink holding Robyn's hand? Now, I'd skate the ice and imagine her hand in mine. I saw the smile that told me she *loved* what she was doing. I could see my mom gracefully gliding along, keeping time with the music, or holding up one of the younger children. Then, laying my memories to sleep, I would thank God that there were still little hands for me to hold.

I did not respond to Verma Harrison's January letter right away. In addition to the difficulty of finding uninterrupted time in my busy household, I needed time to digest all that she had written. But I continued to pray for her.

Sometime in February I wrote back. I wanted to encourage her faith in God as much as I could and manifest the love that He had so generously poured into my life. As I wrote that letter and subsequent ones, I felt God leading me to include certain things, such as Scripture, that would point her to Him. The idea that helping her find healing and wholeness in Him was something God desired from our contact was a current that carried my thoughts to the paper as I wrote.

Her second letter was dated April 28, 1997, and I was encouraged that she seemed to be continuing to move forward in God instead of embracing her old ways.

> I had so much pain and hurt, Mrs. Griffiths . . . It was so easy to drift with the current, and so now it's very difficult to be returning against the stream; but with God's "streams of mercy" flowing through my life, I'm being restored to fellowship with Him. I thank God for granting you a powerful, spiritual gift of ministry.
>
> My heart is no longer insensitive to the Word of God. Have you ever heard the saying, "The heart of every problem is a problem in the heart"? I'm learning so many spiritual lessons through the book of Hebrews.

In May of 1997 I was asked for the first time to go to a church other than my own to share what God had allowed to happen in my life and to talk about the good things that were beginning to grow from it. I was willing to speak because I wanted to witness to the magnificence of God's great and awesome love, both in carrying me through the storm and in enabling me to reach out to Verma (I was also beginning to feel comfortable calling her by her first name).

Driving home afterward, I felt a mixture of renewed grief and excitement. It had been emotionally painful to open the door and step back in time, retelling the story of what happened to my family. Yet I could not deny the fire that was burning in my soul for the Lord and His people. I had seen a glimpse of what God was going to do with this terrible story. Many people had been touched that day. That was not surprising, for it's a touching story, a sad story. But people were more than emotionally moved. They saw God in our story. They saw His power, strength, and compassion. And they were drawn to Him.

I could not help thinking of where it all stemmed from. "Unless a grain of wheat falls into the earth and dies, it remains by itself alone; but if it dies, it bears much fruit," says John 12:24. God was causing life to grow from the seeds that had been laid to rest in the ground. The seeds of my mother's and Robyn's lives.

The whole way home I cried, thanking God for the opportunity and ability to speak, and thanking Him for my dear loved ones' safety in His presence. And again, with all the longing within me to have them back, I prayed that those who had heard would find some healing through the telling of our bitter story.

· · ·

All around me I saw evidence that winter was removing its gray-brown coat. Cheerful spring flowers were giggling and wiggling in my garden as if they contained some silent secret about the surprises summer would bring. Robyn's tulips and hyacinths were beautiful and painful to see. Warm spring breezes of May carried upon them hints of June. The world around me was unveiling itself for summer. And as June approached, a sickening feeling came with it, for it brought the worst memories of all.

I've always loved June, with the finish line for our school year in view and vivid color bursting out in gardens all around the neighborhood. This June was different. How I wished that we could just tear that

month from the calendar! As much as I tried to tell myself that one day
was the same as any other day without Robyn and Mom, I found that
looking ahead toward June and the first anniversary of their passing was
like looking at the horizon and seeing dark, ominous clouds drawing near.

As soon as the date read June, the shallow breathing of the post-
crash days returned. I lost my appetite again too. The visual things in
my world that used to convey beauty to me were now stabbing me
with reminders of my final days with Robyn. The garden looked and
smelled just the same as it had one year before. The warm breezes,
the sunshine filtering through leafy trees, spilling its light in patterns
in my yard—all so similar to June of a year ago. This was the day I
bought Robyn her last bunny while we were Father's Day shopping.
This was the day, the hour, we watched a video together and had
time alone before she left on the trip. This was when . . . that was
when . . . oh, how I wanted to run from it all. But there was no skirt-
ing the inevitable memories. Bill and I had to walk through them.

On Friday, June 27, I went to the cemetery with my friend Kim,
who had also lost a child several years before. We planted flowers at
the grave and had our own little worship service. We cried and sang
songs of God's ability to help us and heal us, recognizing His awesome power over death. It seemed appropriate to me that I should be
planting *living* things for this anniversary. When we were finished, the
spot looked pretty. I wanted it to look nice for the next day when my
family members would gather there.

The next day, the first anniversary of the crash, the sun was shining, just as it had been a year ago in both New York and Nebraska.
In fact, my father had asked that we all be there at precisely nine-
thirty New York time, the moment of impact. Every subsequent year
this has become his ritual. Grief was thick, tears flowed, hugs were
long and strong, and the disbelief that any of this tragedy had actu-

ally happened was renewed to previous levels. And I was thankful that the family tensions around our decision to forgive the woman who had gathered us here were not present.

. . .

To my surprise, I received another letter from Verma on June 28, exactly one year after the crash. Getting her letters, I discovered, was soothing to my soul. Perhaps they somehow gave some meaning to my loved ones' untimely deaths. I began to feel that she was a prize I had won through this very costly confrontation with our enemy, Satan, the father of lies, the author of death. In it, she said,

> I don't blame your father at all for being angry. The very last thing I want to do is hurt you more. Just like I don't want to hurt Jesus more. I am praying that your dad will be able to forgive me. 42 years . . . [this was a reference to the years my parents had been married]. Sometimes I feel like I can't live with myself another day, especially when I'm out and around older couples . . . I'm truly sorry to all of you . . .
>
> Thanks so much for your kindness and words of encouragement and quoting scriptures to me. I have overcome and if Satan feeds on our doing our own thing, then I plan on starving him! . . .
>
> God is awesome, thanks for showing me His love.
>
> > Through the power of Jesus
> > Christ our Lord,
> > Verma Harrison

Before I had the chance to write back, I received another letter from her, dated July 4.

You are on my mind always . . . Everyday . . . I think of you all.

God is my place of rest. I have no other. In my entire life, and still to the present day (except for my sponsor/counselor), there wasn't anyone close enough for me to confide in—with anything. Maybe there was and it was just me who wouldn't trust enough.

I know you must truly be missing your mother and baby. I feel that nothing I say will ever make up for what's happened. I understand fully and completely all the anger directed toward me now . . .

I need your father's forgiveness. It weighs heavy on my mind. My Creator knows my heart and with Him as my witness I stand to tell others that truth is on the inside and I'm not just performing religiously. I've acknowledged and will no longer make excuses . . .

Mrs. Griffiths all the things you spoke of in your first letter, I'm experiencing. It feels great to finally be purified by God's grace and mercy. I also know now that Christ can forgive any trespass . . .

I didn't write my next letter to Verma until October. We were still walking through the grief and trying to learn how to move on without a part of us, without Robyn. During those months, though, particularly in light of her letters to us, I had a quiet assurance that God Himself was leading her. I had tried to encourage her in the truth, which is the way to healing. But God needed to cause the growth. At the same time, I sensed that I was to continue to water the seed of faith when the Spirit led me.

Here is part of my next letter to her, dated October 13, 1997:

June was a real difficult month. There were so many reminders of the way it had been a year ago. From the warm air and flowers to my last memories with Robyn—and my mom, too. It was like living it again.

Sometimes I feel like I'm not really here, even though I am physically here. June and July were like that. Now I am back into homeschooling my four younger children and my oldest started high school in a Christian school.

My husband is okay and not okay. But he's not able to talk about Robyn much at all. It's too hard still.

My father, well, he's having much difficulty. You will probably see him at the end of this month. I understand your sentencing date is October 29th. Know that you have my prayers and the prayers of our church family here. We pray that God will have His way. He knows what His plans are for you. Keep trusting in Him. He will not let you down. He will not break His promises to you. He is a present help in times of trouble.

I pray that you will keep your heart fixed on Him. When everything around us seems to be crumbling, He is a Rock that will not be shaken. I pray that Romans 8:28 will give you courage and hope. Please remember that in spite of your own thoughts and feelings, in spite of any human's judgment about you, you are totally accepted by God if you've let Jesus into your heart. His word alone is truth—and the truth will set you free.

I think the day is coming when I will fly to Wyoming to meet you. What do you think of this? I am praying about it.

Please write to me when you can. Oh, by the way, a little blessing I learned when I read a library book recently about the Navajos:

> In beauty may you dwell,
> In beauty may you walk,
> In beauty may it rain on you,
> In beauty may your corn grow,
> In beauty all around you may it rain,

In beauty may you walk,

The beauty is restored.

In the love of Jesus,

Cindy

. . .

As I had mentioned in my letter, Verma Harrison was to be sentenced on October 29. She had been convicted of two counts of vehicular homicide and DWI. The homicide charges had been reduced from manslaughter, which meant that the minimum she would serve was five years and the maximum ten years.

Two months earlier, in August, we had received a letter from a probation officer from the court in Nebraska where Verma was to be sentenced. The letter informed us of the upcoming sentencing and stated that a presentencing investigation was being conducted. It invited us to write to the judge to express what was on our hearts or to let him know what kind of sentence we thought she should serve, or both. All of my mother's immediate family received such a letter and responded. Naturally, my side of the family (meaning those outside my literal household), and especially my mother's family, wanted them to lock her up and throw away the key or, better yet, just give her the electric chair.

Bill and I had some hard thinking to do. We were in a position where our opinion would, at the very least, be heard. Would our input be consequential? Would letters from the victims' families bear any weight at all in the judge's decision? That was one factor to be considered. Another was the fact that Bill and I were getting to know Verma through her letters. We believed she was not the same woman she had been before the accident. She was in counseling/treatment programs daily, and we believed that she had become someone who would, given the opportunity, take what she had been given and help others. In fact, she already was. On several occasions she had spoken to groups of people about the dangers of drinking, and she had told of her desire to return to her Native American people to try to help those who might accept her help and learn from her experience.

Bill and I believed that it was our job to forgive and the judge's job to judge. When Bill was asked what he thought was fair concerning punishment, he said that "fair" had nothing to do with any of this. "What's fair is that we get Robyn back and that the devil goes to hell. Someday, both will happen," he said. "But right now, nothing is fair for anyone."

Because we had forgiven Verma, we had no hunger for revenge on a human being that needed to be satisfied. We were free of that. We did pray for her, however. I had prayed nearly every day since I first contacted her that God Himself would have the final say concerning her sentencing. Since I believed that He had a plan for her as well as for us, I beseeched Him to work through the justice system to bring about what was best. I did not ask Him that she be incarcerated, and I did not ask Him to keep her from it. I did not claim to know what she needed. My mission was to help her in any way God led me in the hope that the tragedy would be used for good.

As I considered what we should write to the judge, I wondered what would be the responsible thing for us to do. We are citizens of the kingdom of God, but we are also citizens of this country. A country with laws that are there for our protection. Verma had broken those laws. And if perchance the judge decided against a lengthy jail time, what kind of message would that send to others, especially young people: "Hey, it's okay to drink and drive. It's even okay to kill somebody. No big deal, we'll forgive you. All will be forgotten." Sometimes love requires tough measures. I love my children. I forgive them when they have done wrong, but I also punish them to teach them a lesson.

While I grappled with all of this, a Bible story, told in the gospel of John, came to mind. A woman was caught in the act of adultery. According to the Law of Moses, she should be stoned to death. The Pharisees and teachers of the law dragged her before Jesus and asked Him what He thought should be done to her. Whether they were trying to trap Him (again) by His own words or they honestly wanted His advice, we are not told. But we are told that Jesus' response was, "If any one of you is without sin, let him be the first to throw a stone at her." One by one, beginning with the older men (had they acquired more wisdom?), they dropped their stones and left. Jesus then asked the woman where her accusers were: "Where are they? Has no one condemned you?" No, she said. "Then neither do I condemn you," Jesus said. "Go now and leave your life of sin" (John 8:3–11 NIV).

Jesus preferred to change the woman's attitude, which would change her actions, rather than punish her. Revealing the heart of God, He forgave her offense and told her to leave her life of sin. Sin breeds death. He wanted her to live. And if something lives, it brings forth life.

As I thought about this story, it seemed to me that Jesus was interested in having this woman be whole. What really spoke to me, though, was that He did all this here on planet Earth, not in some ethereal existence where everything is love, love, love, and angels float around playing on golden harps, singing lovely songs. Her accusers wanted to execute her. And they would have been in complete *compliance with the law* to do so. Yet Jesus gave her back her life with the exhortation to bring forth what was good. If that was Jesus' way, then it would be my way too.

Verma was not our enemy; evil was our enemy. She had forsaken alcohol the day of the accident, and she was now facing and dealing with issues within herself that had fueled her anger and made her want to drink. She was turning away from the kinds of thinking that had led her to depression and destructive behavior. She was in counseling and had even been helping others to find healing before they killed someone's family members.

God doesn't wait for us to be perfect, but He does want us to be willing and teachable. Verma was both. As a result, Bill and I saw her as someone who would promote what was good and right to others who were in ignorance. That was what she wanted to do. And she had her own pain to fuel her and propel her forward as well as gratitude to God for saving her life.

Did we believe in fairy tales, thinking that she could change? Were we naïve to believe her? Some accused us of this. But for us it all came down to God's being God. Bill and I knew all about His love and power. We knew what He had done in our lives for the previous twenty years. We knew what He could do in Verma Harrison's life. Yes! It could be done! She could be a harbinger of hope to those living in the darkness of despair—as she once was. People are certainly more apt to listen to words of guidance from those who have walked in their shoes. Verma was someone who could walk into the prisons of the mind and soul, where she once lived, and show others the way out. If she did this, and she was already doing it, she would be fighting the same enemy that we were fighting. And this enemy, who was responsible for death and evil, including the deaths of my mother and daughter, would have fewer hosts to prey upon and propagate his hellish desires.

Bill and I also believed that she could do good things behind prison walls. But our hearts' desire was to see her go back to her people, on the reservations, and bring hope to them.

Yes, we would appear foolish to some. We knew that. But we would be fools for Christ. Jesus' first disciples said the same thing of themselves. We wanted to trample upon the head of our true enemy and, even from the depths of our pain, see God work unending good out of this immensely vile sabotage of human life.

After much thought and prayer, we sent this letter to Justice John D. Knapp of Nebraska:

Dear Justice Knapp,

My name is Cindy Griffiths; my husband's name is Bill Griffiths. We are the parents of Robyn Griffiths (DOB 12/12/84) and the daughter and son-in-law of Janice Nicolich. Robyn and my mother, Janice, were brought to their deaths while driving through Sidney on June 28, 1996. My father, Joe Nicolich, was there too, as he was the driver.

I am writing to you today in regards to Verma Harrison, who was driving the vehicle that crashed into my parents' car on Interstate 80. I understand her sentencing date is approaching quickly, and we wanted to let you know our thoughts.

It's a little hard for me to know where to begin. To try to describe the agony of losing our precious daughter and mother is not something we can easily do, for the pain runs so very deep. It's beyond anything we've ever experienced. It's as though a major tidal wave—a tsunami—has crashed down upon us and sent us tumbling and spinning in blackness, agonizing blackness. I described it at one point to someone as being tortured unceasingly without the repose of death . . .

My daughter, Robyn, who was born on my birthday nearly 13 years ago, is the second of six children and the first of two girls (my youngest, now five years old, is a girl). She was—it is difficult to write "was" when referring to her—but she was a very special young lady who graced the lives of many with her gentle, caring spirit. She was mature for her 11 years: helping with household duties and with caring for the little ones. She'd intervene when her brothers didn't get along and she helped to create an atmosphere of peace. She'd offer comfort to a sibling who felt misunderstood. And she'd be found every day playing mom to her baby sister (who was three at the time we lost Robyn) by playing with her, reading her stories and the like.

In our family of six children, we teach the older ones to help with and care for the younger children. Robyn rarely complained. In fact, there was little else she preferred over spending time with her baby sister. All of her siblings loved her dearly, so naturally they suffer—unnaturally. We suffer because we love. I've told them this. It hurts so much because we loved so much, and we still love so much.

The shock of my daughter's sudden and violent death has reverberated throughout our families and our local and church communities. Robyn had several close friendships, but we've learned that a large number of girls considered her to be their "best" friend. She had a very loving way about her that caused her to seek to include others, especially the ones that were shy or on the periphery. And Robyn and I were very close. I am not going to describe my relationship with her except to say that I don't think it gets any better than what we had.

I have to admit that I am tempted to go on and on about this child because I cannot see her sweet freckled face any longer. My eyes are now denied their maternal right to watch the sunlight dance on the blonde highlights of her brown hair, or the wind tease her flowing locks. I cannot feel her in my arms any longer, yet I remember her soft skin and wonderful hugs. I do not hear her playing with her brothers and sister, and our piano seems to sit in a sullen silence, wondering why her gentle songs have ceased. Where other moms can talk to their 12-year-old daughters, I now can only talk about my memories of mine.

And then there's my mother. We were very close. She was not

just my mother, but my friend. Always, it seemed, giving, loving, and laughing. She was wonderful to me and my brothers and our children. She had many interests and even had a special "something" for Native Americans. She loved their art (definitely their jewelry) and sympathized with their history. I find it interesting that Verma Harrison is 100% Native American.

Well, I felt the need to share these things. Now I want to focus on Ms. Harrison. Although we despise what has happened at the hands of Verma Harrison, we do not despise the person, Verma Harrison. I cannot remember if it was the first or second day when we learned the driver had been intoxicated with a blood alcohol level of .19, but I remember thinking, *My God, what happened to this woman that left her with no sense of self-worth, self-respect, self-esteem? What happened in her life that caused her to think so irrationally and behave so irresponsibly? What has driven her?*

I felt from the beginning that she probably had a lot of problems and needed a lot of help. I was going to write to her to see if I could help. Knowing that God hears when we call upon Him in truth, I fasted and prayed for three days asking God to give me insight into Ms. Harrison so that my letter would be effective. Early in November of '96 I wrote to her to tell her that I didn't hate her, but wanted to help her. I explained to her my reasons for my perspective and my forgiveness: for they are found in the Bible and are the fruits of a relationship with the Lord, Jesus Christ, and by faith in His Word.

Ms. Harrison wrote back to me—to all of our family. She wrote a very long letter. A letter which confirmed my impressions of her while writing my first letter to her. Indeed, she suffered much abuse at the hands of irresponsible adults during her growing-up years, including sexual and alcohol-influenced abuse.

Now, I am a believer that we need to take responsibility for our actions. We need to make our choices for good or for evil, for life or for death, in all our daily actions. There are many people, I think, who love to blame their parents, their siblings, their teachers, baby-sitters, or the lack of enough candy in their Christmas stockings for their depressions and woes in life. I've been one of them. These folks need to get a grip, it's true, and start making lemonade with those lemons. However, they need to be loved and helped along the way to hopefully reach that point. And then they still need to be loved. And I believe love never fails.

Some have said we are foolish for taking this stand. Some say she's carefully scheming with her lawyer to pull our heartstrings for the very purpose of my writing these things to you. Yet I say (1) it was I who wrote to her first, and (2) we've made contact twice with her pastor; she's been in attendance, since the crash, at a local church, and we've contacted the pastor to discuss her actions and faith. And (3) even if her story weren't true, I would still have the satisfaction of knowing that I did the right thing in case it were true.

In her letters . . . she has expressed remorse for what she's done. I think it is not only remorse for the consequences of whatever might be coming to her, but remorse over the injury she has caused this family. We believe it is real. We believe she is waking up and trying to make steps towards a better way of living. As I stated previously, we've made contact with her pastor, who confirmed what she had written to us, and more. What we've learned is that she's been in counseling two times per week at the minimum. She's been in an intensive discipleship/rehab program with a group called Overcomers Outreach, which is an offshoot of their church. She has been actively involved in reaching out to others who have addictions, telling them of her life, telling them what happened on June 28, 1996, telling them of love and forgiveness and healing and hope. We don't want any of this to end! She wrote and told me how she was about to graduate from college with a degree in business, but wants to change that so she can counsel women. She believes she has something to give now. We want her to have the chance to give it away.

We've been warned that those awaiting sentencing are on their best behavior because they are very scared. And while we can believe that, we still have reason to believe that Ms. Harrison's rehabilitation is genuine, and that her desire to counsel other women who are suffering with the abuses she's received or inflicted upon herself is real, too.

Other families I've met that have lost loved ones due to alcohol did not seem to understand my point of view. But when I suggested that if she's telling the truth, she may be able to reach other alcoholics before they kill someone's loved one, they saw that maybe some good could come out of it.

Justice Knapp, there's been an awful lot of pain and suffering: my husband and me and our children, my brothers and their families, my dear father, who's been a very broken, hurting man, and the many, many others in Janice's and Robyn's spheres of influence. If any good could come of this, we are all for it. We want to see Ms. Harrison have the chance to make good with her life and the lives of her children, and we want to see her reach out to help heal those hurting women she calls "my people."

I don't claim to know all she needs right now. She broke the laws of our land, and I don't know what's in store for her because of this. We want you to know that we consider her an ally and not an enemy if she is going to pursue what is good and right. If she does this, she'll be fighting the true enemy with us, which is evil itself. And that battle is won one heart at a time. Let her influence others so that perhaps even one other mother and father, daughter, and son-in-law will not have to weep the bitter tears we've wept.

Thank you very much for letting us have our say and for considering our thoughts.

Respectfully,

Cindy Griffiths

Bill Griffiths

We sent our letter with a request that it be read into the record during the sentencing proceedings, since we could not be there.

. . .

On October 29, I spoke at a women's group about a half hour from home. They had asked me to speak about God's faithfulness to us in the storm, and His unending love, which reached out through us to Verma. When I returned home, there was no word about what went on in the Nebraska courtroom. All I knew was that my dad was there with his sister, who lived in Colorado. I didn't even know whether our letter had been mentioned; the judge could have denied our request to have it read into the record.

That night as I lay in bed wondering what had happened in Nebraska, I prayed simply, "Lord, what happened today?" Then I fell asleep. I woke up around 3:15 A.M. after having a vivid dream about the courtroom proceedings.

Later on that morning we heard from our lawyer. What he said confirmed the dream I had had. He told me that the judge was going to lock her up—that is, until our letter was read. The judge personally read it aloud, into the record. The reading of the letter was the last thing to take place before Verma was sentenced. The judge then sentenced her to probation with random drug and alcohol testing. The judge had clearly—

and this was stated from the bench—let her off because of *our* wishes.

I couldn't believe it. Humanly speaking, it should not have turned out that way. She should have been locked up for a long time. But somehow our letter had influenced the judge. It had to be God's doing. And my belief was reinforced that God must have plans for Verma Harrison outside prison bars.

A few days later, we received this letter from her:

Nov. 3, 1997
Dear Mr. & Mrs. Griffiths:

I greet you in the Name of our Lord Jesus Christ, whose name was glorified in the courtroom by Judge Knapp on Oct. 28, 1997!

There's no greater love than God's. My feelings and gratefulness are inexpressible towards you and especially to my Savior, Jesus Christ. I will not forget you, all of you, or what happened, ever.

My journey in a new life has begun. Even six days afterward I'm still in awe! I could not believe my ears when I heard my sentencing. I could barely stand or even walk! That feeling stayed with me for at least four days! I cried, and cried, praised God, and cried, thanked God for your hearts and His Love through you, and cried, and cried, and cried!

I'm telling you the truth . . . I have never had this kind of freedom before in my entire life! Not just free from prison bars but free of everything I was in bondage to! I know the peace and joy you speak of, His perfect love. I know, I know, I know! Praise God! Praise Jesus! Praise His wonderful Name!!

He was glorified for all to hear! . . .

You've shown us so much Mr. and Mrs. Griffiths . . . We can't ever thank you enough. I just praise God. I will serve the Lord. We will serve the Lord. Norman [her fiancé] devoted his life to God back in March of this year . . . Our children speak God's name more and more. They're so eager to please God, it's beautiful! . . . We rejoice now because we belong to God and He has given us the desire of our hearts.

I can tell you that if it weren't for your forgiveness and love, I wouldn't be alive. If it weren't for your beautiful letter, I wouldn't be home with my babies, I would not even know God.

We pray daily for you and your entire family, brothers, aunts, uncles, cousins, and especially your father. I can't explain how I feel for all your hurts. Just please know I hurt along with you. I wanted so much to hold him [my father, at the sentencing] and apologize, beg for his forgiveness . . . I couldn't contain myself, it was an experience to feel so many things at one time, I was torn apart.

I'm doing better, but my mind still operates like I'm still under pressure. I still rush around as if I'm running out of time. I catch myself still wondering what my destiny will be or if my children will be alright with someone else . . . Most of my time though . . . I'm crying. I just don't think I can ever thank you enough . . .

I couldn't believe my eyes when I read your last letter. I prayed that I would, if there were ever a chance, meet you in person. To hold you . . . to feel you're real . . . that you are a child of God. My prayer would once again be answered when that takes place. I look forward to the day, Mrs. Griffiths.

Through your act of kindness, forgiveness, and love, my entire family's lives are beginning to reflect upon God's love.

Thank you. I love you.

Love in Christ,
Verma J. Harrison

P.S. Our Thursday devotions are going great . . . The women in our group have a new light in their eyes from my life. God is awesome!

CHAPTER 28

WALKING THE BRIDGE

(CINDY)

In November 1997, I took a big step. I decided to phone Verma and speak to her personally for the first time. I also decided that I should make plans to fly out and meet her. Our two lives had been joined by the tragedy. I grieved over the loss of my daughter and my mother; she grieved over our loss and the fact that she was the one who had caused it. She might be free from prison bars, but as she told me, she will never be free from her past. She will live with what she did for the rest of her life. And we will live with the result of what she did.

I called her pastor and got her phone number, and then I worked up the courage to dial the phone. Finally one Friday when Bill came home from work, I told him I was ready. We waited until our kids were in bed, so we wouldn't be distracted. However, when it was almost time to call, I said to Bill, "I don't think I can do it." Suddenly, I was afraid to hear her voice. Holding her inanimate letters was one thing; hearing her speak and breathe was another. *Why do I want to put myself through this?* I wondered. *I can't hear Robyn and Mom, but I'm going to hear her voice?* No. This call could lead to some of the good fruit God promises to work out of bad situations for those who love Him. Who knows what kind of spiritual doors could open for Jesus and close on the devil?

So Bill and I went to our bedroom to place the call. I asked him to bring another phone into the room so I could see his face while we talked to her. I didn't want to be alone. The line rang once, twice, three times. Bill was sitting on the floor with the other phone to his ear. I said to him, "For Robyn, for Mom, for Jesus." He nodded. My heart was racing, but I couldn't hang up.

"Hello," said an adult male's voice.

"Hi . . . this is Cindy from New York. Is Verma there?"

A moment of silence just hung there. "Uh, yeah. Hold on. I'll get her."

I held . . . and held . . . and held. Whatever trepidation I had gone through to call her included at least preparation. She was being caught completely by surprise. The moment was upon her, and I could only imagine that she was staring at the phone receiver, unable to pick it up.

"Hello?" asked a little voice, sweet as a bird, but unable to hide her fear completely.

Nervously we started with small talk. Then she started crying and thanking us for what we'd done for her. Between sobs, she told us that she was sorry. At one point she said, "I love you guys." To which, Bill responded, "We love you too." Hearing Bill say that made *me* cry.

We talked and cried and prayed for about an hour. I had a sense that heaven was eavesdropping on both ends of the wire and was rejoicing that once again love had triumphed over hatred—all because of *His* great love. Jesus' words kept running through my mind: *If I be lifted up from the earth, I will draw all men to Myself.* As we are drawn to Him, we are drawn closer to one another.

We discussed the possibility of my going to Wyoming in December. But afterward, when I had thought about it more and discussed it with my friend Elaine Harwood, our pastor's wife, I realized that December was just too soon. Elaine suggested I wait until after the winter so there'd be time to plan. Also, the weather would be better then. In a way, I didn't want to wait that long, but I knew she was right. Bill agreed. Elaine volunteered to go with me since Bill wanted to stay home with the children.

The winter months brought more exchanges of letters with Verma, and our friendship deepened. On January 21, 1997, she wrote,

More and more I see him [Norm, her fiancé] getting closer and closer to God. Even in the way he speaks, he refers to what the scriptures have to say. His family back home have even asked what has happened to him. They're amazed at how much more caring and loving he's become. A side they claimed they haven't seen since his brother died, about twelve years ago. I praise and glorify God's name for all the changes He's made in our lives!

Our love has deepened because of God's love. We both see what that's all about through the two of you and your family. I know Norm was touched by the Holy Spirit when I told him both of you prayed with me over the phone. It was powerful! We cried and talked for a very long time. It was a breakthrough. Walls came crashing down! Praise God! . . .

God spoke to us and many other people through you. We lift you up in prayer always and we want you to know we love you very much. Our testimony has had some impact on a lot of people and you know something else? I am overcoming the shame and guilt of telling my story, because I want people to know JESUS LIVES! He cares and He forgives and loves us all! We no longer want to be just hearers of the Word, we want to be doers of the Word. There's no turning back now, ever.

Her letters, like the following one, often brought tears of joy to my eyes. I could see the transforming work of my God by the things she was learning. And I thanked Him for it.

The devotion I read this morning made me realize even more just how much more powerful is God's love.

You see, the enemy still tries to come in and destroy my ability to love myself after what I did. More and more, I'm putting all of God's commandments in my heart and talk about them continually, and impress them on my children, and others.

So far, I've learned there are three basic loves: love of God, love of neighbor, and love of self. I feel I make a difference with the first two, but the third is difficult for me. I know that if I'm able to love myself and be comfortable with who God made me to be, I'll have my life characterized by joy, praise, and enthusiasm. I ask myself daily if I'm able to reflect the joy of the Lord. But I feel I'm not able to love myself.

I know I love God and everyday wherever I go I find reasons for giving Him thanks. Always I want to be less selfish and be able to set aside some of my needs in all my relationships. I found that when I let another person's needs take precedence over my own, it's a sub-mission that I base on reverence for God. Out of respect for Him. It's a daily challenge for me to do this . . .

I can't help but think of your father and how your relationships with your family have changed because you helped tremendously in keeping me with my family.

Each day I read God's Word, I learn more about His patience, forgiveness, joy, justice, kindness, compassion. The list goes on and on. When I think of you and your family, I feel I could almost feel the tensions of your lives. This makes me sad, but I remind myself that in spite of the pain, frustration, and anger, family is still God's gift. I see more that the caring, nurture, and confidence that comes from being seen at our worst and still knowing that we belong, is His gift to us . . .

Without the joy of the Lord I know I'd be unable to function properly. I can do nothing well without His joy.

The following is the first of nine pages, which I wrote in response on February 7, 1998:

You've told me how much my letters have meant to you, but I want you to know that *your* letters mean so much to me. Every time I've received a letter from you I end up crying and thanking God.

Bill and I didn't know if we would get to see the fruit of God's touch on this side of eternity or not. He's not only letting us see some of it, but is even using us to reach out to others because of what's happened. Yet, I suppose the whole world could come to know God, and in this mother's heart it would never be enough to justify Robyn's early departure, but it does my heart good to hear people tell me how God is using this in their lives.

Most of all, dear sister, my greatest joy (yes, God gives me joy in my sorrow) is to know that you are doing well in the Lord. So when you let me know how God is working, and how much He means to you, I cry with thanksgiving to Him who holds all life and death in His hands.

Yet even if you were still miserable and in darkness, I'd try to be your friend. I would want you to live for Him, and not for my sake, for truly, your debt is to God.

Also in that letter I gave her the details of my travel arrangements to Cheyenne. In February, I exchanged the plane tickets that had been purchased back in 1996 for our trip to join Robyn and my family for my brother's wedding in Salt Lake City. Now they'd be used to unite me with the one who had caused me to be separated from my mother and daughter for the rest of my life. I cried over the plane tickets in my hand before I made the phone call to the airlines, but as with everything else connected to the tragedy, I was conscious and thankful for the redemption, ironic as it was.

In many ways, Verma Harrison and I were very different, both in personality and in life experiences. Yet we had something huge in common: the need to be pulled out of the black, raging storms of our pain. As I grabbed hold of the Lifesaver in the midst of the tossing sea, I helped Verma to grab hold, too, knowing that only He could sustain us both in our fight to keep our heads above water. And because the Lifesaver is also the Life Giver, I continued to care about her well-being, and because I cared, I wanted to meet her.

I didn't believe that meeting Verma was going to bring some kind of healing for me, as some have suggested. Forgiveness—and the resulting healing—was already happening. It just seemed to be the next step I was supposed to take. Just as writing all those letters to her seemed to be the right thing for me to do, so our meeting seemed to be a door I was supposed to walk through. The time was right. I was ready.

· · ·

For two weeks before my trip to Cheyenne, I didn't sleep well. I wanted to go, but I was scared too. I'd wake up in the night after just a few hours of sleep with the sense that something really important needed doing. Then I'd remember what that was—meeting Verma.

Inevitably I'd have difficulty falling asleep again. As a result, I ended up excited, nervous, and *tired*.

A few days before we left, several unanticipated things happened. Elaine and I were to leave early Thursday morning. On the Monday before that, a new friend of mine, Deborah Tadova, told me that she had a connection with someone who worked in the News 12 TV newsroom (our local Long Island station), and she asked whether I would want him to know about our trip.

Bill and I talked it over and decided that if people could hear about my trip and why I was doing it, perhaps the story could be used to help others find *their* road to forgiveness. We hoped this would be the case and prayed for God to continue in His promise to work all things for the good.

An interview was arranged for Wednesday, and Tuesday night I once again had trouble sleeping. I'm not sure which I was more nervous about, doing the News 12 interview or meeting Verma. It was probably a toss-up.

On Wednesday, anchorman Scott Feldman and a cameraman came to our home. Since it was spring break, Stephen, our oldest, now attending a private school, was home with us. I was glad we were all together. Our little (okay, not quite *little*) family was being given an opportunity to show something of the love of God on local news. We told the kids this was part of our revenge on death for taking Robyn and Grandma.

The interview lasted about an hour and a half, and Mr. Feldman was a gentleman off camera and on. Bill and I appreciated his sensitivity. We'd never been quizzed like that before, and it was difficult talking about Robyn, knowing that perfect strangers would be listening. Robyn and the events that followed her passing were such personal parts of us. Now we'd be sharing her and the circumstances surrounding her death with many. It felt strange and right at the same time.

After the interview was finished and Bill returned to work, Deborah asked whether we would be interested in being interviewed by *Newsday*, a Long Island newspaper. She had a friend there too.

I was beginning to feel as if a whirlwind had just blown into town and lifted us up in it. At first, I was concerned about letting the paper get involved. Would the paper relate the story truthfully? Many regard Judeo-Christian beliefs as the last burning embers of a threatening fire that dares to contradict popular mores and must be stamped out as soon as possible. This story could not be told without reference to our Lord and Savior, Jesus Christ, because without Him there would be no story. Would the paper honor that? Or would it distort the story into something biased or inaccurate?

I called Bill on the phone and discussed it with him. Once again, we came to the conclusion that this could work out for the best. If the trip were reported accurately, then more people would hear about the love of God.

One thing that encouraged me not to be afraid was something I remembered from Billy Graham's autobiography, which I had read that winter. In it, he wrote positively of some of his contacts with the press, telling how he saw that God could be glorified through media exposure. I would believe the same. But with that belief went prayer. Prayer that God Himself would handpick the reporter who would work with us.

Almost within the hour I received a phone call from *Newsday*'s Carol Eisenburg. "How would you feel about me coming out to Cheyenne *with* you?" she asked. And she wanted a photographer to accompany us. I hadn't expected a request like that, and I was thinking it through even as I responded. I explained to her the nature of what I was about to do and that I was going to be emotionally vulnerable on the trip, as were the other people involved. Anyone with me needed to be sensitive to that and could not be intrusive. Carol reassured me that both she and the photographer would be very careful. Bill and I discussed her proposal and agreed to have them join us.

That Wednesday afternoon, as we waited for the TV interview to be aired, our electricity went out. The power plant, which was less than a mile from our home, was bellowing gigantic flames. The kids and I wondered whether we'd get to see our interview on News 12 that night after all. Then I realized that no one else from our area would get to see it either.

The interview was to be aired first on the five o'clock news, and then throughout the evening on subsequent news programs. I prayed that God would protect the people who were working to put out the fire and restore power. Then, at 5:02, by our clock, our power was on. I smiled heavenward at the timing.

Later on, my son Stephen said that he thought that God could be using the fire to get more people to watch the news that night. Folks would tune in to learn about what happened at the power plant and then they'd hear about God's love from our story. Only God knew.

That night, weary and excited, I packed my bags. As I did, I wondered what the future held. *O God, what do You have in store for me in Wyoming? What plans do You have for this story that You are broadcasting through the TV news today and through the written news when I return?*

CHAPTER 29

FACE-TO-FACE

(CINDY)

Elaine and I had an early flight out of JFK airport on Thursday, April 16. As the plane left New York behind and headed westward, so did my thoughts. My stomach knotted as I pondered what I was about to do, and although I wanted to go, I also had a growing sense of dread. I tried to anticipate my meeting with Verma, but it was hard to imagine what might happen. Oh, I could well imagine the emotions that would be involved, but anything else was difficult to foresee. Off and on during the hours of the flight I prayed about what was ahead, prayed for Bill and the children and the friends who were helping out while I was gone, and chatted with Elaine.

In Denver, we met up with the *Newsday* reporter, Carol Eisenburg, and the photographer, Michael Ach. We rented a car and began the hour and a half drive north to Cheyenne. During the ride, Carol began her interview.

It was awkward at first. I was going to talk about very personal things with someone I didn't know. But Carol, armed with her writing pad and tape recorder, worded her questions very carefully and sensitively.

Soon I was speaking freely about my girl, my Robyn, my sweetie of eleven and a half years. How, on a sunny day in June, she went away for a nice family gathering, and only days later was gone. It had been a sunny day . . . Dad was driving . . . they were hit from behind . . . they needed the Jaws of Life to get her out . . . Mom was gone too . . . Mom and Robyn were buddies in life and buddies in . . . Dad was unconscious . . . a concussion . . . broken ribs.

Going there was emotionally difficult. Every time I told about it, I relived it to a degree. However, it was not difficult to find the doorknob to the door behind which my memories were stored. All I needed to do was give the knob a quarter of a turn, and everything came spilling out like a too-full closet.

My life had changed radically the moment my brother told me about the crash. I would never be the same. This was *my* experience: the pain, and the hope because I believed the future held great things in spite of the pain. Even *because* of the pain. I tried to convey these things to the reporter.

The photographer sat in the front seat next to Elaine, who was driving. When he snapped his first shot of me, I found it disconcerting. The click of the shutter seemed loud. It shattered my thoughts, bringing me back from abysmally painful memories. But what I had already experienced and what I was about to experience were much bigger than having someone buzz about me with a camera. Even if that someone happened to be a professional photographer. It just didn't compare. And after that first uncomfortable shot, it didn't matter.

We arrived at our hotel in the late afternoon, and I called Verma to let her know we were there. She was nervous too. I was exhausted, and I decided that it would be better to wait until the next day for our meeting. Already emotionally vulnerable, I didn't need further physical depletion.

Next morning, after spending time in our own personal Bible reading and prayer, Elaine and I discussed my upcoming meeting with Verma. I told her that I was apprehensive about it. Part of me was afraid. I was afraid to see her face, and I was afraid to touch her hands. The very hands that were on the steering wheel that drove her van into my family, my Robyn. I was afraid that when I saw her, all the grace I had had toward her would suddenly disappear and I'd be left standing there with hatred in my heart.

Elaine reminded me of the Bible text that says if a man or woman comes to Christ, he or she is a new creation (2 Cor. 5:17). She reminded me that I was not going to meet the same Verma Harrison who was responsible for the deaths of my mother and daughter, for she had a new heart now. A new will and power from the Lord of all creation to empower her. We spoke of God's love again and again, and I soon found peace of mind and anticipation of good things in my heart.

We met Carol and Michael in the lobby. Having dinner together the night before had afforded us all the opportunity to get to know one another better. We piled into the rental car and set out for Verma's house, about fifteen minutes away.

En route, we discussed how we were going to proceed. They wanted to enter Verma's house before me so they could witness the event from the beginning. At first that seemed a strange request, but I soon realized that it would be the only way for them to report it accurately. They were two gentle souls who did their best to be sensitive to me and to the situation. Carol said she would not ask any questions during my time with Verma; she would just watch and listen. She would resume the interview later. Michael said he would try to be like a fly on the wall, staying out of our way.

Coming from New York, we were all amazed at how much sky we could see in every direction as we drove through Cheyenne. That Wyoming sky seemed to be watching, too, as we turned up Verma's suburban street.

Okay, here's her house, I thought. I felt queasy. I wanted to just *do* it and get past it. Elaine, Carol, and Michael left me alone in the car and went into the house. I didn't watch them go in. I closed my eyes and, breathing heavily, spoke to God. I thanked Him for bringing me to that point, and I sang a song to Him. Then figuring they'd had enough time to set the camera up and get situated, I stepped out into the brisk Wyoming morning air.

The sun was shining as I made my way up Verma's front walk. A friendly black cat greeted me at the stoop. I stroked its fur and said hello. Then I climbed the two steps to her door. I didn't look through the glass of the outer door. I just opened it and stepped inside.

In my peripheral vision I saw Elaine, Carol, and Michael off to the side. But my eyes locked onto Verma Harrison, standing in the middle of the room, waiting to receive me.

She was a little shorter than my five-foot-four-inch frame, and I thought she looked much different from the picture she had sent me. Her pretty face, dark eyes, high cheekbones, and long dark hair could not hide her frightened anticipation. I don't remember physically walking toward her, but suddenly we were in each other's arms.

"Oh, Cindy," she cried.

I cupped her face in both my hands and looked her squarely in the eye and said, "My sister, I love you in Jesus." Then we hugged and softly cried, and cried and hugged, and hugged and cried. We held each other for a long time. She held me so tightly I was starting to sweat in my winter jacket. Trembling, she whispered, "Cindy, I'm so sorry . . . I'm so sorry," again and again. She said, "I can't believe what you guys have done for me . . . Thank You, Jesus," and, "I just want to hold you so I can get more of God's love."

While we embraced, a cacophony of thoughts filled my mind. Primarily, I felt a sense of accomplishment and gratefulness. I could feel God's love pouring through me, and His presence was euphoric. Reaching out to this woman had saved her life, and in turn she was reaching out and saving other lives. What more could I ask for? Under the circumstances, I had a total answer to prayer. But holding her was bittersweet. The arms embracing me were the same arms that had maneuvered the weapon of death off the road and into my family's car. I could see Robyn and my mom and dad. The accident, as I imagined it, played over in my mind, and the grief renewed itself.

No. I didn't want to dwell there and allow the real enemy to creep in and mar this moment. No way. To do so would be to resist God, and I didn't want to do that. Couldn't. Wouldn't. To love her would be what Robyn would want, what my mom would want, and more important, what God wanted. Love had reached out to this desperate soul and was changing her life.

Then Verma started singing slowly and thoughtfully in her native Navajo tongue. I recognized the melody and simultaneously began singing in English. Nothing else could have been so appropriate, and we sang together, "Amazing grace, how sweet the sound that saved a wretch like me. I once was lost, but now am found; was blind, but now I see." Heaven's grace had comforted us when neither of us thought we could ever be comforted after the accident. And it was heaven's grace "that brought us safe thus far." Amazing grace had united our hearts. No wonder the Bible calls God's kingdom the unshakable kingdom! What earthly government could bring about such unity? None!

I felt I was in the midst of a miracle, and I could not contain my gratitude to God. I took hold of Verma's hand and raised it with my own toward the ceiling and sang "Shout to the Lord." Through tears of sorrow for the past, relief for the present, and joy for the future good that would come from our union, we sang together,

> My Jesus, my Savior, Lord, there is none like You.
> All of my days I want to praise
> The wonders of Your mighty love.
> My Comfort, my Shelter,
> Tower of refuge and strength,
> Let every breath, all that I am,
> Never cease to worship You.
> Shout to the Lord, all the earth, let us sing!
> Honor and majesty, praise to the King.
> Mountains bow down and the seas will roar
> At the sound of Your name.
> I sing for joy at the work of Your hands.
> Forever I'll love You, forever I'll stand.
> Nothing compares to the promise I have in You!

We finished our song with tears and with laughter. The ice was broken. Then Verma and Elaine and I talked for about an hour while Carol sat quietly on the ledge by the fireplace, and Michael skirted around us taking pictures. Verma talked a lot about what it was like for her in the beginning, at the time of the accident, and then when she got my letter and subsequent ones. She spoke slowly and thoughtfully, stopping every so often to regain her composure. Elaine spoke to her intermittently in her loving, pastoral way, encouraging her to move forward.

After the time together at her house, Verma and her older boy, Josiah, took us to an AA meeting where Verma had participated. With the permission of the person in charge, Verma and I went to the podium at the front of the room. Verma told the group who she was and what she had done. She tearfully spoke about the accident and my Robyn and mother. From my place behind her, facing the room, I thought again that this was a miracle in the making. Here we were, testifying to the power of God's love, together. I couldn't believe it, but there we were. I was awed.

Verma then introduced me, and I spoke about the biblical principle of sowing and reaping actions in our lives. I also spoke about our inability to sow the right seeds apart from the power that God supplies, and I encouraged them to pursue Him.

Afterward we went to a restaurant for lunch. Neither Verma nor I could believe that we were actually sitting down at a table across from each other with nothing unholy between us. We expressed that to each other. We were so aware that we could break bread together (share a meal) because of the One who said, "I am the Bread of Life." Because He was *broken* for us, we could *become one* in Him.

We returned to her home, where Elaine and I met her other children, Jessica, who was nine, and Braden, seven. (At that time, her two younger children did not know about the accident.) They were delightful, bright kids. Later, we met Verma's fiancé, Norman.

In the evening, we attended a church service with Verma, Josiah, and Norman, where Verma and I once again told our story. We sang out our praise to the Worthy One, lifting our hands high in triumph over the darkness of sin and hatred, grief and depression. We were overcomers.

The AA meeting and the church service were the first of several church meetings and support groups where we would share our story.

Verma's joy in having Elaine and me with her was obvious. At one point someone asked her, knowing she didn't have a happy childhood, how old she felt that day. With beaming face and tear-filled eyes, she responded, "Oh, about seven!" I felt a lump in my throat. In many ways, her childhood had been stolen from her. Yet God was restoring what had been stolen. Indeed, she was experiencing the new life that Jesus died to bring her. She was His baby now. She couldn't turn back the hands of time and erase her past—oh, how I wish she could—but the Lord could work in her and make everything new. And He was. New beginnings.

When we returned to our motel, we learned that Cheyenne's CBS affiliate had tried to contact us several times. News 12 from Long Island wanted to follow our story and had contacted the Cheyenne station to cover it. However, Elaine and I felt at that point that a television camera and crew would be too intrusive. Also, we didn't think it wise to let people in Verma's community see all of this on TV. We didn't want to put her children into a situation where they might find out about the accident from other children or be picked on in school. Verma would tell them when she was ready.

That night as I lay in bed, I thought of the events of the day. Then I realized that the date was April 17, the date Robyn had written on her loft, the date I couldn't figure out any special meaning for. I did now.

I fell asleep, satisfied, and slept soundly through the night.

• • •

The next day, Saturday, I would visit the crash site, about a hundred miles east of Cheyenne. I wanted to find something to leave next to I-80 as a memorial to Robyn and Mom, so I suggested we look for a garden shop.

Elaine and I found one without much trouble, and I roamed around the store trying to find something that reminded me of Robyn. What I found was a dark gray stone rabbit, about eight inches tall, with a cute bonnet on her head, and in her paw, nestled up against her tummy, was a little basket full of wee flowers. She looked sweet, and she reminded me of the many rabbits Robyn had owned and loved. I also found a white oval rock engraved with the words *I LOVE YOU*, with a heart in place of *love*. Then we looked for a plant.

I wanted something with pink or purple blossoms, for pink and purple had been Robyn's favorite colors. But this was April in Wyoming, and the store's supply of outdoor plants was limited. I settled on a small shrub, indigenous to the area. It would bloom in late June, said the clerk, and its blossoms would be white, like snow. Late June. Blossoms like snow. *Of course*, I thought. *It will bloom in late June for* Robyn Snow.

Then with everything in the car, including a borrowed shovel and a large plastic jug filled with water, we set out for mile marker 65 on Interstate 80.

It was another sunny day. The air was chilly, and the sky was dotted with cumulus clouds. It was hard not to notice them; there was so much sky. As Elaine headed the car eastward, my spirits sank downward. The dark, oppressive cloud descending upon me was nothing like the cheerful, buoyant puffs in the sky. *Why am I doing this to myself?* Yet I knew I couldn't be this close and not go. I was compelled as if the very ground that was beneath her when she breathed her last was beckoning me.

The nearer we came to the place where the accident happened, the worse I felt. Carol and I had been talking in the back seat, but I reached a point that I could not talk anymore. Elaine put a cassette tape into the tape deck for me. It was filled with uplifting songs about God's love and nearness—the very same tape I had sent to Verma. I made myself sing along with the tape, not because I felt like singing, but because I wanted to remind myself of the truth in the midst of everything around me that was causing me such pain.

We had been driving for about an hour and a half when someone said, "There it is!" Mile marker 65.

Since we were on the eastbound side of the highway, we continued until we came to a place where we could cross the highway. Then we doubled back on the westbound side. All the while, I was staring at the road, looking for the tire marks that my brother told me would still be there. I was imagining their car traveling along this same stretch of highway almost two years ago. Then someone said, "There they are!" referring to the two makeshift crosses my brothers Scott and Ray had erected about thirty feet off the shoulder, several days after the crash. I began to cry, feeling pain for my siblings. How horrible it must have been for them to stake these memorials in this lonely middle of nowhere.

I suddenly could imagine the collision. I could see my mother unaware that death was an instant away. I could see my baby Robyn singing her song to God with her headphones on. I could see my father preparing to put the transmission into "park."

We pulled over.

Getting out of the car, I started to walk around, just looking, trying to find anything that would connect me to what my family had gone through here. I noticed that the mile marker on this side was gone. Then I found it, bent and lying in the grass. I did not find any tire marks. They were supposed to be from my parents' car. There never were brake marks from Verma's.

I could hear the crash with steel crushing, glass shattering. I could see the last breath of life leave the lips of my mother and daughter. I grimaced and wanted to scream.

Then I walked over to the crosses made of sticks, feeling every step. They stood about two feet high and had been upheld by a pile of stones at their bases. One of them was nearly on the ground. I found a stone the size of my hand, dropped to my knees, and began to pound the fallen cross back into the ground in an upright position. I hate you, Death. *Wham!* Satan, you're gonna get yours! *Wham!* Just you wait till Jesus comes back! *Wham!* Jesus is Lord. *Wham!* He is Lord over death! *Wham!* Robyn lives! *Wham!* Mom lives! *Wham!* Death is not the end! *Wham! Wham! Wham!*

Dad . . . the bodies . . . the people *I love.* How I missed them. I'd have given anything to have them back. But I couldn't. I was spiraling downward into grief. And after a while, I realized that I could not stop the flood of emotion. Through my tears, I started to sing songs of God's sovereignty over all. In between singing, I sometimes spoke aloud, even shouted, timeless truth from the Scriptures. I was addressing an unseen enemy, and Scripture was my weapon. After a while, I sang songs about God's love and care for me, and I was comforted. Elaine came over and, putting her arm around me, joined me in song.

After what seemed like a long time, the emotional upheaval subsided, and I looked out across the bleak Nebraska plain north of the highway. I imagined it in the summer when the grass was greener. It was probably a pretty, tranquil place. For a minute, while there were no noisy cars or trucks moving on the highway behind me, I heard a bird singing. I thought it might be a meadowlark.

When there was a break in the traffic, I ran across to the center median, where my parents' car had come to rest. I found furrows in the ground, obviously made by their tires. Among the tufts of wintered grass, I found a hair pick that I thought was my mother's and some pieces of broken Tupperware. My mom had so much Tupperware from being in the business many years, I was sure the pieces had come from their car. I sat down and combed through some of the grass with my fingers and found shards of what appeared to be the dinnerware set my mom had intended to give to Rob and Katie for a wedding gift. I couldn't believe it. After nearly two years! Some pieces were half embedded in the now hardened soil. Some were as large as my hand.

I continued to look around. I found bits and pieces of their van. Nothing major, of course; anything major had already been removed. Their deaths were all around me as everything seemed to scream at me of the violence of the event. In disgust I threw the pieces of dinnerware onto the ground and stated, "Let's leave this place of death." I had had enough.

I crossed the westbound lanes to return to the shoulder and our car. I took out the things I had bought at the garden shop and carried them to the crosses. I dug a hole behind the crosses and planted and watered the small bush. Then I set the stone bunny down in front of them and pressed it into the ground.

Finally I took up the engraved stone. I held it in my hands for a moment and ran my finger over the engraving: *I LOVE YOU.* Yes, I love you, Robyn. I love you, Mom. I wish it didn't have to be this way. I know you two see the end of this now, from where you are, but I cannot. Someday this will all make sense to me. My trust is in the One who could have prevented this. He will not disappoint those who rely on Him. But I can't stand this separation. It's killing me. Oh, Ma, I want to talk to you. Ma, Robyn's gone. I can't do this, Mom. I don't *want* to do this. I just want you here with me. Both of you.

I laid the stone near the bunny, and then I was finished. It was time to leave.

On the way back to Cheyenne I couldn't speak. I was paralyzed by the reality of where I had just been. But when we were almost there, I saw a beautiful sight, which helped me to refocus. Since we were headed westward and it was getting late in the day, the sun was low in the sky ahead of us. Suddenly the golden radiance of the sun seemed to be flowing upon and over the many cumulus clouds, spilling forth its brilliance like liquid gold, dripping to the earth below, bathing earth and sky with luminescence. The effect was glorious. It wasn't just a pretty picture; it was magnificent. And for a few moments it made me think of what the glories of heaven must look like.

The beauty before me brought warmth and comfort to my heart, reminding me, as Elaine had at the site, that mile marker 65 on Interstate 80 was not just a place of death and departure; it was also a place of entrance. Entrance for my mom and Robyn into a realm that would make the most glorious natural beauties of this world appear pale in comparison. My two dear ones, my ladies, were jubilant in the presence of the One who had created the breathtaking scene before me. And I would be there, too, someday.

· · ·

On Sunday morning, we went to church with Verma. The pastor knew I would be there with her, so he made time for us to share a bit of our story. I had choreographed a dance to a song about God's love and ability to see us through life's darkest night, and I performed it for them. Then Verma had someone pop in a music track to a song that she said had been very meaningful for her since the accident. She was going to sing it, and she wanted me to sing it with her. The song was "Breath of Heaven."

After Robyn left us, one song in particular was constantly on my mind. It actually is a prayer, which Amy Grant sings on her *Home for Christmas* CD. The song, from the point of view of Mary, the mother of Jesus, speaks of her probable emotions and pleas for help. I identified with the lyrics and sang them often that first summer. Again, not because I felt like singing—it was a plea for help.

When I would sing the parts about Mary having a baby inside, I thought of my pain inside instead. And just as she knew she was bringing forth a very special life from God, I knew that life, intended by the Creator, would come out of the painful burden I carried and the lonely path I walked.

Now here I was in Cheyenne about to sing a song with Verma Harrison. A song that was very special to her and to me. A song that had become the cry of *our* hearts. And it was "Breath of Heaven." We sang it together, each pouring her heart out to the One who always hears.

On Sunday afternoon, Carol and Verma and I went to lunch together, and Carol interviewed Verma. That was when Verma told Carol virtually her whole life story. Some of it was hard to tell too. Telling her story to a newspaper reporter was a big enough step for Verma, but even bigger was the fact that it was for a "white man's paper."

Getting to know Verma Harrison has greatly broadened my understanding of Native Americans. She's shown me how hard it can be for her people to trust the white man—and with good reason. But Verma told her story to the reporter that afternoon because she had decided to trust God above and beyond any person, believing that this would ultimately bring glory to God. And I was proud of her for it.

We spent Sunday evening at the home of Verma's counselors. The couple are overcomers themselves. They've known what it is to be enslaved by addiction. And for years they've been helping others find their way out of the black cycle. Even before my first letter came, they had been trying to help Verma find healing and strength in God. Now, they were like family to her.

Sunday night, when we returned to our motel, I let Carol read the letters Verma and I had sent to each other. I had been copying all of my letters to her, thinking that someday when my children were grown, they might want to check out the evolution of our relationship for themselves. Carol had asked if she might read them, and with Verma's consent, I let her do so.

On Monday morning, Elaine and I bade good-bye to Michael and Carol, who were flying back to New York. It was a little sad for me to say good-bye. It had been an incredible weekend, and these two strangers had been drawn into the inner circle with us. Michael said that he felt he was witnessing something of the miraculous. And both told us how moving the experience had been to them personally. I had revealed my heart's agony, my tears, and my hopes to Carol. Now, our paths would separate.

On Tuesday morning, under a clear Colorado sky, with the Rockies that Robyn never did get to see rising just west of us, Verma and I embraced one more time before Elaine and I caught our flight from Denver. I felt protective of Verma. I didn't want to say good-bye. I wanted to stay out there and help her grow. In a sense, she was my baby. That labor I experienced so that Robyn would be born into heaven, her death on earth, which I died, too, had brought forth this new life. Life in the heart of the one by whom it all had happened. I thought of the great paradox of the situation. And I remembered Jesus. It was our sins that nailed Him to the cross. We are guilty, guilty, guilty. But through His forgiveness, the guilty ones are cleansed and then become the very recipients of His great love, both in this life and in the one to come.

We shed some tears once again, promised that we would continue to stay in touch, and then we parted.

Hours later, Elaine and I arrived back in New York. We had been gone for six days, but each day had seemed like a week. So much had happened. So many thoughts and emotions. It had been a good trip. My mission was accomplished. Or was it?

CHAPTER 30

THIRSTY SOULS DRINK

(CINDY)

Early Sunday morning, our friend Dennis O'Dowd called and asked if we had seen the paper yet. We hadn't. Bill and I didn't subscribe to the Sunday *Newsday*. Dennis went on to tell us that our story was on the front page. "And," he said excitedly, "it's four pages long!" He told us he'd bring his copy to church for us.

Front page. That sounded important. I was surprised that it was featured so prominently. During the Cheyenne trip, Carol had told me that *Newsday*'s readership was 700,000. "Wow!" I'd said. "That's a lot of people." With the story there on the front page, who knew how many could be helped with the message of the freedom that love and forgiveness bring.

Later that morning, when I entered the building for Sunday services, I saw that someone had placed a copy on a table near the entrance. I glanced at the cover. Sure enough, there was a picture of me kneeling by the crosses beside Interstate 80. In bold letters the headline read, "Her Road to Forgiveness." But it was afternoon before I finally had some undistracted time to sit down and read the whole article. As I did, my eyes welled with tears. It was a good piece, well written and sensitive. Seeing my mother's and Robyn's pictures in the paper like that was difficult, but good.

That night we received several phone calls from people who had read the article. One woman, a stranger to us, said that after reading the article she realized she had to forgive her ex-spouse after twenty years of bitterness. If we could forgive such a wrong done to us, she said, then she could forgive this man too. We also had a call asking us to do a TV interview.

Markus Wilhelm from Doubleday Publishing also called. Markus, Bill's friend, fishing partner, and fellow archery enthusiast, had just read the *Newsday* article. It was a powerful story, he said, and one that the world needed to hear. Aware of Bill's writing experience, having contracted to publish *Malchus*, Bill's first novel, he asked if we would write our story in book form. Obviously we agreed.

In the weeks and months after the news article came out, we heard many, many reports of how it was being used in various settings as an example of forgiveness. From dinner tables to offices, from classrooms and Sunday schools to church services, our story of tragedy and redemption had sparked interest as an inspirational tool.

One woman called to say she had a framed picture that she wanted me to have. She said the story had impacted her so much, and the picture represented our story so well, that she had to find a way to get it to me. It just so happened that the next night I would be doing a TV interview in the same town where she had a meeting, so she said she'd drop it off for me. When I arrived for the taping, I found waiting for me a two-by-three-foot framed picture of a light-house shining forth its light into a violent storm. The caption read,

"FAITH—With a guiding light, all obstacles can be overcome." My heart was touched that a complete stranger would go out of her way to give me this.

Not all reaction was positive. My father was extremely upset by the article. Also, several newspaper editorials attacked our decision to forgive. A couple were from people who had lost loved ones much the way we had. They were angry that we had helped Verma Harrison and accused us of interfering with the law.

On the positive side, I started getting more and more invitations to share our story with various groups, sometimes weekly. Occasionally Bill joined me.

It has been a tremendous privilege to be welcomed into many assemblies across Long Island and elsewhere and share our testimony. But it is always difficult to speak of what happened. I spend my days trying *not* to think of what happened in June of 1996. But when I tell the story, I deliberately go there. I must go there. I must tell of the hell, or I cannot tell of the glory. When I get to the good parts, the parts about love and forgiveness and healing, my strength is renewed, and I'm glad I'm there. And many times after speaking at a meeting, I have the opportunity to pray with the people in attendance. Doing that is an honor for me.

Always, after I tell the story, folks come up to me to tell me how thankful they are that I have shared it with them. Always, too, there are tears. Some have lost children. Many are going through tough times and are struggling to keep believing that good will come of their situations. And there are always those who are wrestling with their own bitterness toward others who have offended them. Many, many times people tell us that our story crashed their pity parties and set them free from feeling victimized, giving them the desire to look past the hurt and move forward in their relationships and in life. All of these testimonies are like precious jewels to me. Jewels that are being stored in the very place where so much was ripped out of my heart.

. . .

Along with the speaking engagements, we had done several local TV and radio interviews. But in October of 1998 we had a truly surprising phone call from the *Oprah Winfrey Show*.

Back in January of that year, a friend had suggested that I write to Oprah about our story. (This was before I had gone out to meet Verma.) I wrote a brief letter to Oprah describing what had happened to us, and when the *Newsday* article was published, I sent that in.

We heard nothing, and I didn't concern myself with the prospects of anything happening. Then in October, Oprah's people called to say they were doing a show on apologies and forgiveness. Would we be interested in flying out to Chicago if they wanted to use our story? We chatted for a while, and then I said, yes, we would do it. They told us they would get back to us.

Wow! This is unbelievable! I thought. But deep down inside I'd had a hunch this would happen. I was surprised and not surprised. The sense that we had a message that was important to be told and heard was now magnified. Bill and I felt privileged, but sad at the same time. We felt a duty, but it was a sad duty.

Well, they did want to use the story, and just a few days later they sent a crew to our house for an entire day to interview and tape for the show. The following week, they flew us out to Chicago to tape a show with Oprah before her studio audience. They also brought Verma from Cheyenne.

As Verma and I sat and talked with Oprah, I could see that this delightful woman, in the midst of all her celebrity, is a person who is also truly a seeker of truth and love. When she asked how I could ever forgive Verma, I told her that I had simply given Verma what God had given me—love and forgiveness.

Our segment ran fifteen or twenty minutes. During the course of the show Oprah mentioned to us that thirty-three million people watch her show worldwide. And I thought the *Newsday* audience was big!

Above all, Bill and I appreciate the platform that Oprah gave us from which we could share our message of hope and freedom. The response has been remarkable, especially considering that nothing was mentioned on the show about where we live. People regularly come up to me and tell me that they were helped by the message they heard on the show. One day in the doctor's office a woman, who recognized me from the show, told me that she had been quite busy feeling sorry for herself until she heard our story. She had recently lost her husband and needed to forgive God. Now she has a new, less weighty perspective.

More than a few have told me that they or someone they know had taped the show and are using it as a teaching tool in a classroom or study group or as a way to help friends and relatives. A friend called to let me know that forgiveness and faith were the topics of a discussion her daughter had with a group of women from her graduate school sociology class. They had all seen us on Oprah's show and were very interested to know more about us and our faith. The notion that someone could forgive such a transgression committed by an irresponsible stranger solely out of principle was unfathomable, given the natural human response. Most objectively agreed that extreme forgiveness must be accompanied not only by a belief in God, but also by God Himself. The discussion then turned to how one truly gets to know God.

Shortly before we taped with Oprah, and then throughout that week, I had a real longing for my mother. I wanted to talk to her about all that was happening. I wanted her to marvel with me. I wanted to see the sparkle in her eyes and the beam of her smile as she looked upon me approvingly. Just prior to doing the show, I had spoken to a women's group, most of them around my mother's age. On the way home I said to God sarcastically, "It's nice that I could be with these ladies today. There I was talking to everybody else's mother, and I can't even talk to my own."

A couple of weeks after being with Oprah, I received a letter from a woman who had been a friend of my mom for years. She lived in Texas and had seen our story on Oprah's show. In the letter, she spoke of my mom, saying that based on the kind of woman she was and her faith in God, she "just knew" Mom was very proud of me. She was the second person to tell me that while I had been missing my mother so deeply. It was a balm to my aching heart.

. . .

All of these opportunities, of course, cannot bring back my daughter and my mother. But if I cannot have Robyn and Mom back, then I will be glad for the good that will come to others because of them. Their deaths have become like seed that is being scattered, producing growth in other lives.

After I first heard the news of the accident, my prayers were that life would grow out of the death. But in the midst of my desire to see this tragedy redeemed in any way possible, I want to be God's tool, not the other way around. And I want to follow God, not *make* gods out of precious principles. I've heard about pastors who have lamented in hindsight that they went off and served their ministries instead of their God, running ahead to build kingdoms and ministries that were of their own hands and thus having only the form and appearance of God, but denying God's timing and power. This is a real danger, according to Psalm 127:1 (NKJV): "Unless the LORD builds the house, they labor in vain who build it." Bigger is better only if God wants bigger, and only He knows that.

What if God's plan does not include me seeing any more fruit on this side of eternity? Will I then become bitter against God for not answering my prayers? Will I be depressed over it? The fact is, I need to be at peace with whatever comes. I don't want to hold anything in my heart higher than God's will. I will continue to pray that good will come from all the pain and suffering, and I will thank God whether or not I see that good.

Thus far, the good does not measure up to losing Robyn. I don't see how it ever could. All the good that has come from this situation seems but a drop in a bucket compared to what it was like losing her. But I know the day will come when every tear shall be wiped from my eyes and my joy will completely overtake this present suffering. That day, when all of this will make perfect satisfying-to-me sense, will be the day when I get to be with Robyn and my mom again in the presence of God.

CHAPTER 31

REVENGE OR FORGIVENESS . . .
WHICH IS SWEETER?

(BILL)

I have rewritten this chapter more times than I would like to admit. To be able to safely encapsulate my perspective concerning family strife within the pages of this book where *only* my side can be read, unchallenged, is frightening. No matter what I write, I feel that I will be a bully or "holier than thou." Honestly, my self-righteousness and hypocrisy, not to mention attitude, need as much work as anyone's. Like most people, I often need time to cool off and gain perspective.

Forgiving Verma might seem monumental, but I found it easier to forgive her than to forgive some of the people who have attacked us for our decision. Forgiveness is something I am learning about and frankly am not great at.

What Verma did was easier for me to comprehend. She made a mistake, a big one. No, the mistake wasn't that she killed. The crash and its outcome were the result of her mistake, and she bears full responsibility for that. Her mistake was that she drank too much and then attempted to operate a motorized vehicle. In doing this, she broke the law and, knowingly or not, gambled with precious life. The crash was unintentional. She wanted to escape from reality, *not* bring it crashing down on everyone's head.

Cindy and I did not campaign about our decision to forgive or recommend leniency for Verma Harrison. We knew that the concept of forgiving her might not be easily understood or readily accepted by all. We thought we might get some frowns or disagreement, but nothing like the uproar that resulted from our letter to the judge, especially from some who were so close to us.

At this point I would love to acknowledge those who supported us with prayers, kind words, and good counsel, but after reviewing and rewriting this chapter many times, I find I had to delete them entirely. The problem I faced in revealing those who were with us was that, by exclusion, I revealed those who, shall I say, were not. Although this chapter was at one time full of both, I no longer want to do that.

However, I *will* say that the court, in an effort to prosecute Verma Harrison, had invited all family members to write to the judge, and most did. They had their own strong opinions about what should happen to her. The family was very divided in supporting our position and understandably so. Everyone lost loved ones.

But Cindy had lost a daughter *and* a mother, and the judge was visibly moved as he read our letter aloud in the courtroom before delivering a verdict of ten years' probation. The revenge that some had been longing for, tasting, had been swept away—all because of us and our "fanatical" beliefs.

We soon found that we were traitors. How *dare* we forgive such an act? Some couldn't even speak to us. Their positions are completely understandable, but the extreme emotion of the time led some to say and write things that needed to be judged as "heat of the moment" and not "written in stone." Typically, Cindy had better discernment on that than I did.

I wrote letters in response, only to throw each one out before mailing it. I tend to write these letters in my anger, but fortunately Cindy reads them before they go out. She usually says, "You can't mail that." I stand my ground and tell her that I certainly can, but then I throw them out when she leaves. I would eventually realize that such responses would only become fuel for further accusations and deeper bitterness and a spiritual banana peel for me and others to slip on.

My pastor told me that letters can be one of the worst ways to deal with problems because without seeing gestures or hearing tone and volume, communication can be easily misinterpreted. Phone is better, and in person is best, where a handshake, hug, or kiss can be added.

That was probably one reason Cindy originally felt the need to personally see Verma. I didn't. While I encouraged Cindy to follow her heart and reach out in love, I did not want to put myself through further acquaintance with the tragedy. And the thought of visiting the accident site . . . well, I couldn't even read an obituary, much less go to the actual spot where it happened. But I'd spoken to Verma on the phone and had no problem expressing my love or forgiveness to her. I wished her well and prayed that she continued to heal and help others to avoid similar pitfalls.

But after Cindy visited Verma, resentment grew. Were we insane? Didn't we know who she was? Because of Verma, our lives and the lives of who knows how many people had been irreparably changed forever. Forgiving her was bad enough, but then we had to write that letter to the court, actually rendering the tool that set her free. We were, at best, desperately deceived.

Not long after Cindy returned home from Cheyenne, a higher court overturned the lower court's ruling of probation, citing the prior verdict as overly lenient. No sooner did this new verdict pass than Cindy received a call asking if she had heard the "good news" about her "drunken Indian whore friend." These calls were too common and usually ended with Cindy walking away from the phone upset, repeating aloud to herself, "My fight is not against flesh and blood."

Our hope and prayer were and still are that love will prevail in the end. Until then, we must separate the anger from the one who is angry. To attack the person who is angry would be a devastating mistake, but to attack the anger—yes. Fighting anger with more anger would be like fighting a flood with a garden hose or fire with a torch. Love's first virtue, according to the apostle Paul, is patience. I struggle with patience. I know time to be both friend and foe. Time heals and then it kills. But with the stakes so high, I must force myself to resist the temptation to fuel and ignite hot coals that, if left alone, will eventually disappear.

After Cindy and Verma appeared on the *Oprah Winfrey Show*, both support and bitterness escalated. Oprah herself had been extremely supportive and couldn't have painted our decision to forgive in a better light. During her program, the benefits of forgiveness were displayed as obvious winners over resentment and revenge. In fact, the following week, she replayed her interview with Cindy, along with seven other guest interviewers, as her "best ever" interviews in thirteen years and over twenty thousand guests. Cindy was slotted into a segment at the end of the show called "Remembering Your Spirit." The portion of the show was relatively new and geared to encourage the audience to second-guess what I would call natural thinking or human nature and to consider spiritual principles such as compassion and peace in the hopes of stirring and strengthening a spiritual consciousness to be more alive and reflexive in our day-to-day living.

About this same time, Verma's lawyer managed to appeal the higher court ruling to the state supreme court. Again our letter to the first court was reviewed, and the supreme court judge ruled in favor of the first judge. Verma was not going to jail after all.

The fact that we remained steadfast in our stance was seen by some as a bridge-burning of relational ties, and we received a few knee-jerk responses that, again, should be overlooked for the sake of eventual peace.

The old saying, "Nothing is certain but death and taxes," is not true. You also have to make decisions and live out their consequences. Not to make a decision is also a decision. Forgiving Verma Harrison was a choice we wanted to make, and it was one we needed to make. We were compelled. Someone who is forgiven much has a magnified capacity and ability to love others if she responds to the forgiveness. With so much to gain, we had to take the chance. The fruit of my Robyn's and Jan's deaths depended on it. We could not let them die for nothing.

Bitterness makes this truth impossible to grasp. As far as the world is concerned, normal Christianity, as laid out by its founder, is not normal. Jesus flatly told His disciples that anyone attempting to live a Christian life will find his enemies will be those of his own household, specifically labeling the immediate family. However, there is no indication that has to be a permanent, lasting condition. Sometimes people need time to get past their own emotions to see what is best. I know I had to. At first, love has an uphill fight against anger, but in time, the roles reverse.

. . .

Speaking for myself, I wouldn't be able to forgive any substantial transgression without a belief in God and the devil. Without my faith, I would most definitely align myself with what Hollywood heroes have been teaching me since I was an infant. Vengeance and revenge.

This is not a knock against Hollywood. In the wonderful world of fiction, of which I am a paid member, vengeance and revenge are important tools for creating motivation and suspense. If you're writing a story about human beings, you need to portray human nature. The problem is that sometimes the darker areas of our natural traits are glorified for the sake of a compelling story, and as a result, we are taught the wrong way to act and think.

What would you rather see, *Death Wish*, a movie where Charles Bronson hunts down and takes his vengeance on the killers who raped his daughter, stalking them one by one until they have all paid for their evil actions, or, uh, hmm, let's see . . . what movie has the victim forgiving the assailant because it's the right thing to do? I don't know. I can't think of one. But I *do* know that I liked *Death Wish* and the sequels.

You mess with me and I'll mess with you. That's human nature. Hit me first, and I'll hit you back harder. Much harder. How interesting would *Rambo* be if the title character didn't fight back when unjustly persecuted? I wouldn't have watched it the half dozen times that I have. My favorite Clint Eastwood movie, which is no easy choice because I like them all and know them by heart, is *The Outlaw Josey Wales*. The theme is vindictiveness, and the moral is that retribution pays in the end if you're bad enough. Sweet revenge. It captivates us. And this isn't just a guy thing. What man in his right mind would dare to step on the toes of some of the characters that Sigourney Weaver or Linda Hamilton have played? Even the scariest aliens aren't safe around them.

Yes, as a fiction writer, I know the importance of revenge. Revenge takes a character and puts him in dangerous places he typically wouldn't go, where he does things he typically wouldn't do. The central character of any story has to want something. If the central character doesn't want anything, you don't have a story. One of the easiest things for him to want is to *get even*. Everyone can relate to it.

Revenge works in movies and books, *but not in real life*. Take our friend Clint. In most of his movies we're attracted by his cool, no-nonsense approach to everything. He can down a shot of whiskey, shoot someone dead, spit, say something like, "A man's got to know his limitations," without his pulse rate ever changing. This makes for good fiction. But in real life, people who act like that are called psychopaths and end up in maximum security (or should). We have this incredible desire to fight back, this sinful propensity to hate, but unlike in the movies, in real life hatred eats us alive.

Before I believed in God, if someone had told me that I was going to forgive a drunk driver for killing my daughter, I would have thought he was crazy, and I would have been horrified. My ancestry on my father's side is Welsh, a people of great pride and a sense of honor. My ancestry on my mother's side is English and Sicilian. The English were always ruling over someone, and what island, small as it is, has provided Hollywood with more crime material than Sicily? A place where personal and family honor had been taken to the absurd. An insult could easily cost you your life. Feuds between families could last centuries.

Violence and vengeance are as much in my blood as anyone's. When calamity, aggression, or simple frustration comes my way, my first thoughts are never peaceful ones. Unchecked by my faith, I wouldn't have rested until Verma Harrison had paid. Actually I wouldn't have rested afterward either. That's one of the deceptions of hatred and revenge. It ain't over till it's over, and it ain't ever over because real life is not a movie.

I might enjoy a fleeting time of satisfaction, but soon enough fear of retaliation would come. And then there's the need for the constant reassurance of self-justification to stay the guilt away. But the guilt won't stay away, and neither will the fear. The real enemy will see to that. Guilt and fear are his favorite weapons, after selfishness and pride—the two things that get you going in the first place.

When Cindy and I flew out to Chicago to appear on Oprah's show, more than a few people asked me if I was going to be all right, meeting Verma for the first time. I still had not been face-to-face with the woman who had killed my daughter. Amazing as it may sound, I was unconcerned about how I would react. Forgiveness works miracles. I had forgiven her more than two years earlier and hadn't had a vengeful thought toward her since. In truth, I was concerned for *her*. I had heard that she was fearful of meeting me, and I was looking forward to putting her fears to rest.

Our first evening in Chicago, we had dinner with friends who lived in the city. They met us at the Omni Hotel, where we were staying. (Both the hotel and the dinner were compliments of Oprah.) We had just finished ordering dessert when Cindy motioned to me with her eyes to look to the right. Verma and Norman, now her husband, had just been shown to a table nearby. Verma had no sooner sat down than I was standing next to her.

"Hi, Verma. I'm Bill. It's good to see you."

She looked stunned, and tears welled up in her eyes. Then she stood up and hugged me. "Thank You, Lord," she said a few times. There wasn't much else to say.

I then asked the waiter if he could join another table to ours so they could sit with us. Verma and Norman protested, saying they didn't want to intrude on our company, but we insisted that they join us.

As I sat there at the table I was not troubled. I did not see a woman whom I hated and wanted to choke. Instead I saw someone whose life had been changed, along with the rest of us, through tragedy, and then changed again through love and forgiveness. By showing her mercy, I was able to confirm in her heart, and my own for that matter, that God's love transcended any circumstance. It was a miracle of forgiveness.

CHAPTER 32

VERMA SPEAKS FOR HERSELF

We believe that this book and its message would not be complete without a word from Verma herself. Here, in her own words, is what love and forgiveness have done for her.

To the Nations of the World,

My name is Verma Jean Harvey (Harrison). I'm a thirty-two-year-old First American Indian. I am a member of the Navajo Tribe of southwest Arizona and New Mexico. I am a member of the Redhouse Clan, and born for the Red Running Into Water Clan. I am a mother of three wonderful children and have always been very grateful for my family. My husband, Norman, as well as my children are also of the Navajo Tribe.

When I received Cindy's first letter, I was contemplating suicide, because I could not live with what I had done. In the months following our tragedy, I didn't have faith in a loving God. I didn't have faith in anything or in anyone at all.

I grew up being a very prejudiced, bitter, angry, and shameful child. I had a hatred for all white people for the blanket of suffering and death they spread out upon the Navajo Nation and onto all redskin nations. The government had a direct effect on my family and people through exposing my father and our proud men to the radiation of uranium mining. My father, Phillip Harrison Sr., was a miner, and as a result, contracted lung cancer. He died in his early forties when I was three years old. Our family fought the U.S. legislature on a wrongful death suit for many years, only to be disappointed time and time again. Year after year I watched my mother suffer as she tried to support six children alone. I've twice witnessed the effects of a nervous breakdown, which stole our mother from us mentally.

Having to witness all this hardship firsthand only added fuel to the fire that was started by a "man of God" who practiced his sexual perversion on my sister and me. This was how God was introduced to me, and so my faith had been buried since I was five years old!

As my brothers, sisters and I were shuffled back and forth between states from one boarding school to another, the meaning of a loving home, a family, a oneness, became more and more distant, and life itself was lonely, dark, cold, uncaring, and void. I had no hope, knew no kindness, but I did know grief, suffering, perversion, shame, isolation, punishment, poverty, ignorance, negligence, violence, unforgiveness, and *rage!*

Then, through the outreach of Bill and Cindy, I saw love in a whole new light. It completely changed my views of God and true Christians. It helped me to change my perspectives on white people and their lack of respect and value for our economical and cultural significance. I realized that it wasn't about trying to mold or fit myself into a culture or tradition, as I was made to believe. I truly believed that white skin was evil because people who wore that color helped strip me of myself.

Through our tragedy, I came to understand that I was truly in a spiritual battle, and that my enemies were not human, but spirits of darkness!

An acceptance I never knew began to cultivate and mature, and as that began to transpire, the little girl within me was resurrected from her death. Although I'm a grown woman with a family, I became a child again. I'm not sure exactly how to explain it, but I understand the meaning of the scripture in Matthew 18 where it says we have to become as a child to journey into the land of bliss: "Verily I say unto you, Except ye be converted, and become as little children, ye shall not enter into the kingdom of heaven" (v. 3 KJV).

The love Bill and Cindy expressed to me was immeasurable, and more than words could ever describe or fully express. This type of love cannot flourish or prosper in a human heart without the love of God. It is a precious understanding that is freely offered and given only by Jesus Christ. Through this wonderful family, God has given me the gift of forgiveness, salvation, love, kindness, knowledge, acceptance, a hope and a future, and a new song in my heart.

Today, I live with the knowledge and understanding of where true love comes from, and I offer it freely to anyone who crosses my path in life. I am now committed to sharing with all people, whether they are white, red, yellow, or black. I live with Ephesians 6:6 (KJV) in mind always: "Not with eyeservice, as menpleasers; but as the servants of Christ, doing the will of God from the heart."

I choose to live in freedom from all shame, guilt, darkness, prejudice, hatred, alcoholism, and every lie that kept me bound for so many years! In Hebrews 4:16 (AMPLIFIED), it says, "Let us then fear-lessly and confidently and boldly draw near to the throne of grace (the throne of God's unmerited favor to us sinners), that we may receive mercy [for our failures] and find good grace to help in good time for every need [appropriate help and well-timed help, coming just when we need it]." *The truth has set me free!*

My prayers are that every person who reads this book will be touched by the Spirit of the *true living God* and be forever changed. For those who are experiencing, or have experienced, similar adver-sities, afflictions, and addictions, let me be a living testimony: *There is hope!* We can overcome with the power and light of the almighty God. It is He who has given me the courage to live and be different for Him.

If you have never invited Jesus, the Prince of peace, to be your Lord and Savior, I invite you to do so now. If you're sincere about it, you will experience a new life in Christ!

I pray you will find a new hope, a new peace, a new life, and a new strength through our story. I have, and each day of my life I live in thanksgiving, choosing to celebrate the positive! May God bless every nation, tribe, and tongue.

> Jesus bee iina doo bee
> adindiin biyi,
> (In the life and light of Jesus)
> Verma Jean Harvey

CHAPTER 33

SNOW ON MY BIRTHDAY

(CINDY)

Somewhere in my house is a little cassette tape. A very little cassette tape. One of those miniature tapes used for answering machines or mini-tape recorders. Ours was used for an answering machine we once had. And that particular tape records a message from me to my mother announcing Robyn's birth on December 12, 1984.

The doctor told me my due date was approximately December 24. *How exciting and wonderful,* I thought. *A Christmas baby!* Yet contractions woke me up in the wee hours of December 11. Was it possible that this little package from heaven would arrive as a birthday gift for me? Maybe even make its entrance *on* my birthday, December 12?

I had been told that subsequent labors are usually quicker than previous ones, so I was a little surprised to see that this one, my second, was taking all day. Finally around eight that evening, we were ready to leave for the hospital, but not until a friend came with some vanilla Häagen-Dazs ice cream. My mother had arrived to care for

Stephen, who was eighteen months old, and I was more than ready to unload my cargo.

I went into the hospital a little overconfident. The nurses had made me feel like such a pro when I delivered Stephen. And I'm glad they did. I needed their encouragement desperately. His was back labor all the way, and they helped me believe I could do it. Yea! Labor coaches! Now I faced this second delivery thinking I could handle anything. However, somewhere between Häagen-Dazs and "push, honey, push," I lost confidence and fear took over. I wanted to run from those contractions. *I've had enough of this. I've changed my mind. I'm going home now.* My mind screamed, *I don't want to do this anymore!*

Fear can be a problem for many women in labor. We become pain, or the pain becomes us. We forget that our bodies were made to do this. We can even forget that there's a baby on its way. After that labor and delivery, I learned to *focus* on one contraction at a time, *believing* that my body could do it, and *reminding* myself that a baby was coming at the end of it all. Maybe that's not a great revelation to some, but I had to concentrate on those things or I'd get lost in fear. I didn't realize at the time that I was beginning to learn a valuable lesson in *choosing* what I would allow into my mind. A lesson that I would need to apply in many areas of my life. A lesson that would help me deal with a much greater pain than bringing a child into this world: the pain of having a child leave this world.

• • •

"Happy birthday, Cin!" Bill said as I watched him hold our new baby girl only seconds after her birth.

"Is it my birthday? What time is it?" I replied, relieved that labor was over and thankful that I could rest from it all.

"12:03 A.M., December 12."

Wow! She made it! And only by three minutes. My little girl was born on my birthday! I was thrilled. *Amazed.* Of the 365 days in the year this little one had been presented to me on my birthday. December 12 would no longer be *my* birthday, but *our* birthday.

How beautiful she is, I silently prayed. *Thank You, Lord.* It was a gift from the Father's hand, not only because of the new life but also because of the timing.

Bill and I always had trouble deciding on names for our children. Popularity of the name was not important. We wanted names that were pleasing to the ear and had satisfying meanings. During each of my full-term pregnancies, we would discuss names and always end up referring to a baby name book for ideas. Those times would inevitably end up comical. Various names would remind us (well, usually Bill) of someone or something humorous. So if the first two minutes of name searching were on a serious note, the next twenty would be spent joking and laughing, largely due to Bill's sense of humor. And I enjoyed those times of silliness.

When it came to our girls, we decided we wanted to use words found in nature. Bill came up with Robyn Snow for our first baby girl. "Robyn" made us think of a carefree bird, the freedom of a bird in flight. And we hoped and prayed that our little one would be a person who would be free—free to be herself, and free to give and receive love.

"Snow" reminded us of her birth month, December, and interesting properties that we hoped her character would emulate. For instance, snow, when it first falls, has a quality of purity. We hoped that Robyn Snow would be honest and sincere in her relationships with God and with people, and that her dealings with both would come from pure motives. Also, each snowflake is supposed to be uniquely different from all others. We wanted Robyn to know that she was unique and special. And we liked the idea that snow reflects light. Snow can reflect so much light that people have been known to experience snow blindness where their vision is lost in all-consuming light. We hoped that Robyn would reflect in her life, by knowing the love of God and giving it away, the light of Him who said, "I am the light of the world. He who follows Me shall not walk in darkness, but have the light of life" (John 8:12 NKJV).

My mother told me that I was born in one of the worst snowstorms on record in New York. In fact, she couldn't remember it snowing on my birthday *since* I was born. Well, now there was snow on my birthday again. And there would continue to be so. Not the pristine, cold stuff that poets write about, but a beautiful, warm, living soul whom I would forever define as "my daughter, Robyn Snow."

As we have done with all our children, Bill and I dedicated Robyn to God. I prayed for her life and that I might be the best mother I could be. Always in the days following the births of our children, when I beheld each new little one, I would recognize anew my need for strength beyond my own. As I held this tiny baby in my arms, so fresh from the hand of God, I also held its future in my hands to some degree. This thought blessed and scared me at the same time. I felt privileged to be entrusted with such a responsibility, but I also implored the Designer of life to give me the wisdom and love I would need to be this child's guide. My comfort came in knowing that there was One who loved the child even more than I did and whose arms were strong enough to carry him or her through this life's worst storms.

After Robyn was born, Psalm 121 was on my mind a lot:

> I will lift up my eyes to the mountains;
> From whence shall my help come?
> My help comes from the LORD,

Who made heaven and earth . . .

He who keeps [you]

Will neither slumber nor sleep.

The LORD is your keeper . . .

The LORD will guard your going out and your coming in

From this time forth and forever. (vv. 1–2, 4–5, 8)

As Bill and I dedicated Robyn to God, we not only asked God's protection and guidance for her, but also vowed that we would teach her about Him, praying that He would draw her into a loving relationship with Him. And we asked that her life would be for His glory. We never had a formal dedication ceremony, but in the quiet of our home and hearts we prayed. "She's in Your hands, Lord. Do with her as You will."

• • •

I also have another cassette tape that is extremely bittersweet to me. Several weeks after the accident, Robyn's belongings were returned to us. Her bicycle and some car games didn't survive the crash, but almost everything else did. Her clothes with bits of shattered glass sprinkled among them, as well as her beloved American Girl doll, Felicity, came home. The now broken portable cassette player housing the tape that Robyn had been listening to and singing with when they were hit. My dad told me that he had turned down the radio to hear Robyn singing along with the tape just seconds before the crash.

With palpitating heart and trembling hands, I put the cassette into our tape player to hear what Robyn had been hearing and singing when she left this world. The song was an updated version of an old hymn, "Take My Life and Let It Be." The tape abruptly stopped after the phrase "Take my moments and my days, let them flow in ceaseless praise."

The following are Robyn's last words on earth:

> Take my life and let it be
> Consecrated, Lord, to Thee.
> Take my hands and let them move
> At the impulse of Thy love,
> At the impulse of Thy love.
> Take my feet and let them be
> Swift and beautiful for Thee.
> Take my voice and let me sing
> Always, only, for my King,
> Always, only, for my King.
> Take my silver and my gold
> None of life will I withhold.
> Take my moments and my days,
> Let them flow in ceaseless praise,
> Let them flow in ceaseless praise.
> Take my will and make it Thine,
> It shall be no longer mine.
> Take my heart, it is Thine own,
> It shall be Thy royal throne,
> It shall be Thy royal throne.
> Take my life, let it be, consecrated, Lord, to Thee.

APPENDIX

(CINDY)

From the beginning, people have told us that our faith has challenged and inspired their own. Some have told us this verbally; others have written to us. When the *Newsday* article appeared, we received mail from people we knew and from people we didn't know. Since Oprah's show aired, we have been hearing many more reports that this message is helping people. This is a real answer to prayer, and many of these letters bring tears to our eyes. Here, in closing, are just a few of them:

> Dear Cindy,
>
> I just want to start off by saying that I have only two heroes in this world, Jesus and you. I am a 14-year-old girl and don't think of many people as being "heroes" . . . I know from the things people say about you that you are a lot of other people's hero, too . . . I wondered how you could have so much love in your heart after this

happened . . . My family means everything to me . . . I hope you keep on telling everyone about your story . . . You have taught me to live every day to its fullest, and to love my family with all my heart, but most of all to forgive people . . . Thank you from the bottom of my heart. Keep on touching people's lives!

This next one is from a Long Island lawyer:

Dear Cindy,

This is just a note to thank you and express my appreciation for your tremendous courage and the message of hope which your story brought to me. I was so profoundly touched by what you went through that I read and reread your story countless times. I would guess that there have been moments when you questioned yourself and the decisions you've made—especially in the face of criticism from family and friends.

Please know that I and the many people with whom I've spoken about you believe in you and have learned much from you. My father shared with me how a woman who he visited in a local hospital was having difficulty forgiving a clergyman who caused her terrible pain many years ago. He referred her to your story. I shared about you with my religion class as we discussed the Beatitude: "Blessed are the pure of heart, for they shall see God." You have illustrated that better than anyone can possibly imagine.

I belong to a profession that often seems to be predicated upon vengeance and deceit. This causes me great frustration at times—and I find myself falling into the same traps. Since the beginning of this year, I keep hearing the message "Don't allow another's actions to dictate the way you act," and I've been trying to apply that to my own life. You have certainly inspired me in working towards that goal.

When I first read your story, you were merely a stranger. As I reread the story, I felt like you had become a close friend . . .

Yours is the most profound story I have ever read in a newspaper. It is the Good News for the modern world. You are to be commended for your unparalleled humility and courage. Again, I thank you for lighting up my life. I will be praying for you and your family.

Dear Cindy,

I just read the *Newsday* story about your trip to Nebraska to meet with Verma Harrison. I support you in this 100% and believe that here is where your healing will be.

In my past, I am ashamed to say, I have driven my car after drinking, many times, and have acted irresponsibly in ways that did not hurt others only because they were not in my path at the time. And so, in finding forgiveness for Verma you find it for me.

I also feel for your angry family and understand their desire for her punishment. Please know I think of you often and of Robyn's perennial garden and her love of music, and how immense your loss is and how great your love.

The following letter was given to us by a friend. She saw it posted on the bulletin board at her workplace. The writer of this letter attached a note encouraging other employees to write to the newspaper as she had.

Dear Sir/Madam:

As one who believes that the "Good News" should be spread, and who feels that too often the media is responsible for creating an environment of madness by the proliferation of the "Bad News," may I say Sunday's paper was a job well done.

The article (Sunday, April 26, 1998) of the Long Island woman, Cindy Griffiths, who traveled to Wyoming to forgive the person responsible for the death of her mother and child, was a wonderful example of the Good News. Without support from members of her own family, Mrs. Griffiths' response transcended the ordinary. Motivated by religious beliefs, she also was an example of behavior, which any psychologist would agree, was the step to her own recovery. She will be in my prayers.

The world would have fewer Bosnias, Middle Easts and Northern Irelands if forgiveness could be preached as our gospel instead of revenge. Youth violence for every perceived incidence of being "dissed" would end if this message were taught from childhood.

Thank you for such an inspiring story.

Dear Cindy:

I want to let you know how very much you touched me with your courage and love.

I shall never forget that exact moment when I saw your picture on *Newsday*'s cover, an image that now has forever been absorbed into my consciousness. I literally stopped and read most of the article right then and there. All that day I thought about your "journey." I consider myself to be very spiritual, and challenged by various acts of forgiveness in my own life; yet I could never fathom walking in your shoes and making the decision you have made.

Nor would I have ever thought that I would be given the opportunity to express my sorrow to both you and your husband, Bill, for the loss of both your child and your mother . . . I know that you all must be grateful each and every day that your father's life was spared. May God's grace and peace ever *continue* in your life. God bless you.